WHERE'S SHARAWRAH?

A Truck Driver's Adventure
across the Arabian Desert

Old Pond
PUBLISHING

First published 2015

Published by
5M Publishing Ltd,
Benchmark House,
8 Smithy Wood Drive,
Sheffield, S35 1QN, UK
Tel: +44 (0) 1234 81 81 80
www.5mpublishing.com

A catalogue record for this book is
available from the British Library

ISBN 978-1-910456-00-2

Book layout by Mark Paterson
Printed and bound in India by Replika Press Pvt. Ltd.

Photos by Gordon Pearce unless otherwise credited

WHERE'S SHARAWRAH?

A Truck Driver's Adventure
across the Arabian Desert

Gordon Pearce

Acknowledgements

Thank you to Laura McConochie for her
computer skills, Tessa Cheek for her literary skills
and Ashley Coghill for all your help.

Contents

Terminology

5th wheel – A large fixed plate on the rear of an Artic unit that the trailer can hook on to

"A" frame – The connection of a rigid truck to a trailer

Artic – Articulated vehicle

Bottom out – When a low loader gets stuck on a humpback bridge

Chai – Tea with no milk

Clicks – Kilometres

D8 bulldozer – A very large-tracked bulldozer with a 12' blade

Dolly – Axle with 5th wheel and "A" frame to go under a trailer

Dolly knot – A special knot on a rope to increase pulling power or to hold loads

Flip flop – Open sandals held on by the strap between big toe and next toe

Jacknife – When the trailer skids round and hits the truck

psi – Pounds per square inch

Souk – Marketplace in the Middle East

Suzies – Air pipes and electrical cable connecting truck to trailer, for brakes and lights

Tilts – Canvas cover over a metal and wood framework on a trailer

Trailer pin – A very strong 2½" metal pin under the front of the trailer to hook on to the 5th wheel of the tractor unit

Wadi – A dry river bed

Saudi Arabia, here I come

"These three buttons on the dash engage the three diff-locks; here are the keys."

The White Trux transport manager and I were in the cab of a Mercedes 2632 articulated vehicle that I was to drive at the start of a new job in Saudi Arabia. That was it! He then got out of the cab and made his way back to the office, saying over his shoulder, "Don't forget to give it a thorough service and check all the oil levels."

This was my first day in Jeddah, Saudi Arabia. It was midday in the middle of summer. The sun was blazing down and it felt like being in an oven. With no shade anywhere, I just wilted, unable to think clearly or do anything.

"What on earth am I doing here," I thought. "Now what have I let myself in for?"

The day before arriving in Jeddah I had been at my home in Maidstone, Kent, enjoying a very pleasant sunny day in June. A couple of weeks before, I had read an advertisement in the local paper asking for lorry drivers to work in Saudi Arabia. The job sounded interesting – three months working in Saudi then one month off at home. It was summer 1978 and with the pay at £150 a week plus trip money, and tax free, this promised to reward me much more than my present job. So I phoned the company, White Trux, and was given a time and day for an interview.

I arrived on time to meet Mr. Michael White, the managing director, in his transport yard office near Canterbury. At the interview I was asked what driving experience I had, and my clean HGV One driving license was checked.

I told Mr. White of my three years in the Army with the Royal Electrical and Mechanical Engineers as a recovery mechanic driving a Scammel recovery truck, or sometimes a Diamond "T" tank transporter. One of these towing a 32-wheeled trailer loaded with a 72 ton Conquer tank would have a gross weight of 120 tons. The Diamond "T" only did a maximum of 25mph, and the 24 gears with two gear sticks made it tricky to drive, when fully loaded.

I left the Army aged 21 and in 1959 joined National Benzole delivering fuel to garages in South East London and Kent. In that job I drove all makes of road tanker from small Dennis four wheelers up to their biggest, a 28 ton Leyland or an AEC eight wheelers. I left National Benzole when they moved too far away to Northfleet, and after that worked for three years as an insurance agent. My father had an insurance brokerage business, and hoped I would carry on in the firm. However office work was not for me, I liked the open road.

Then I heard of a job with Asian Transport. Bob Paul took me on as their first driver in a brand new AEC Mark 5 Mammoth Major and trailer. I did seven years from 1966 to 1973 with Astran, as they were renamed, driving mostly to Tehran in Iran. In 1970, I was the first English driver in a Scania 110 to take a load to Doha, Qatar. The truck and trailer had a full load of telephone equipment, cables, crates and plastic ducting tubes. At that time Qatar had no telephones at all. The first delivery by ship had taken two months and most of the delivery was so badly damaged it was unusable. My trip took only two weeks and there was no damage at all. I was rather proud of that achievement.

Five years of European work followed after I left Astran, but the pull was there to go back to the Middle East again. I was very pleased to be getting the job with White Trux. I next had to arrange to get a visa and a work permit for Saudi Arabia. Then I had to have the necessary injections before leaving. When that was all done I was given a one-way airline ticket. Before I knew it, I was on an uneventful flight to Jeddah. At Jeddah airport I was met by a White Trux driver and driven in a jeep to their villa. This was situated on the outskirts of town, about three kilometres from the centre where the shops and marketplace were. Within an hour of arriving at the villa to say hello to everyone I was taken outside and shown this big 6 x 6 Mercedes truck. The midday sun blazed down, and I roasted in my long trousers and shirt. It was so hot.

As I had a look round the Mercedes, the first things to stand out were the big sand tyres which made the whole truck look bigger and much higher off the ground. There was only a day cab to live in on long trips, but the cab was over six foot wide with a bench seat on the passenger side. This was sufficient to sleep across if you moved the gear stick. The radio cassette player worked well, which was to prove a godsend.

Desert Mercs for White Trux

WHITE Trux International Ltd's Middle East consortium has taken delivery of it's first Mercedes 2632 six-wheel-drive tractive unit. It will operate out of ports in Saudi Arabia.

This model, fitted with a standard cab, has a kerb weight of about 9 tons. The next five on order will be fitted with sleeper cabs.

The V10 320bhp engine, driving through a ZF gearbox with eight speeds plus crawler, provides a top speed of 80km/h (50mph).

Two 12m (40ft) trailers will be used in a double bottom configuration to enable the

complete outfit to operate at 120tons gtw.

The 1400 x 20 sand tyres, oscillating fifth wheel, and electric differential cross-lock, which can lock all three axles, should provide mobility and traction on routes in the Abu Dhabi and Dubai areas.

White Trux desert Merc in local paper

Behind the cab was a full width storage box giving lots of room for straps, ropes, jack and tools etc. On top of that was a 150 litre fuel tank so giving 450 litres total with the main fuel tank. All in all, the truck was longer than the average articulated unit and certainly a good tool for the job.

I found a grease gun in the mechanic's store and made a start with greasing the steering, prop shaft and any other grease nipples I could find. Any metal was too hot to touch, so I needed gloves. At least underneath the truck I had a little shade. Within a couple of minutes I needed a break, but every time I stopped to sit by a wall, just as in the Army, there would be a shout.

"Oi, Pearce, get on with it!"

In the relentless sun I wished I had a hat and, being fair skinned, I wanted to avoid getting sunburn. It did not take too long to check the oil and water and to add distilled water to top up the big batteries. Lastly I smeared grease on the 5th wheel and she was ready for the road.

The other lads were used to the hot weather, but for me that first day was a blinder. It took me a couple of weeks to get more used to the heat of the day. It got up to 120° Fahrenheit in the shade by mid-afternoon. One of the lads got an egg from the kitchen and cracked it open on the roof of his truck. Yes, you can fry an egg on a scorching hot cab roof. None of us fancied eating it though!

What I never got used to were the flies. All day long they sought after the moisture by your mouth and eyes. At least the flies go to sleep at night, though. Maybe they have no night vision or are just tired. As evening approaches the flies leave off. Peace at last? No, the mosquitoes take over, and they bite. Trying to sleep at night in the villa there was always at least one buzzing about. How can a small insect make so much noise?

It keeps you awake and you wonder, "Is it a male, or a female?" It's the females that bite! When it stops buzzing, you worry, "Where is it?" Despite having a sheet over you it is inevitable to get bitten a few times each night. To have an evening shower is asking to get bitten even more, which is an off-putter. You seem to get bitten much less after not washing for two or three days! Mosquitoes don't like to work too hard in the heat either.

Sleeping arrangements were any empty bed you could find. It did get a little cooler after two in the morning, but given the choice it was cooler to sleep in the cab of the truck, as long as the engine had cooled right down.

About once a month a man came round with a big tank on his back. By pumping a handle at his side, a fine mist was sprayed from a pipe with a nozzle into all the rooms. It killed all the insects and supposedly their larvae. The place would be mosquito free for a day if you could put up with the horrible smell! The cockroaches didn't like it much either!

In the basement there was a 10' square concrete room that was used as a cold water storage. When the level got low a big tanker was ordered and with a hose across the pavement into a small aperture in the wall, about 10,000 litres of water filled the place to a depth of four feet. It must have cost a fortune to fill, as a two litre bottle of water cost a pound. Maybe it was not pure drinking water. At least it helped a little to keep the place cool, but I never trusted it to drink. It was much safer to drink bottled water or Pepsi to be on the safe side. Water sold at 50 pence a litre but diesel fuel cost about two pence a litre. I worked it out that a 2000 kilometre journey to Riyadh, there and back, cost less than £20 in diesel fuel.

Breakfast was local bread and jam, no chance of a bacon sandwich in a Muslim country! The evening offered a variety of meals. Sometimes chicken and rice, or you could have rice and chicken. The supermarket in town had a good choice of food and actually it was not all that bad. We took turns at the cooking, so some meals were better than others. Usually meat and veg all in one pot commonly known by drivers as Camion Stew (or spew after having too many beers)! With never more than two or three drivers in the villa at any one time, it took quite a time just to meet them all. I was told that there was always plenty of work to do as the docks were overflowing with goods from all over the world.

Behind the villa there was plenty of open ground to park the trucks and trailers. The next two blocks in our road were walled-off waste ground, so there was lots of parking space in the roads dividing the blocks. Just behind the villa a lean-to was the mechanic's store. All work on the vehicles was done in the open, mostly oil changes and a bit of welding. Because of the extra weight often put on the trailers, the springs needed attention more often with a broken leaf or two.

With the other drivers in Jeddah (me in the red jacket)

The tyres were changed when too much steel binding showed; there were no rules to say otherwise. Apart from my Mercedes truck there were six Volvo F88s which were very reliable and nine trailers. One three-axle trailer had a steel floor which could gross 60 tons, this was used for all the heavy stuff like bulldozers. The others trailers were 40' flat beds which had once been tilts. That's canvas over a metal frame that had been used on the Middle East run, with loads from England to Saudi Arabia.

When at the villa with no loads to deliver, we helped the mechanic with whatever needed doing. Sometimes there was no work to do, so to pass the time we each grabbed an oil can and squirted at the flies when they settled within range. A little bit of revenge, and it helped to pass the time. Being at the base meant we were not earning trip money. A trip to Riyadh could earn you £200 for about three day's work!

I had a couple of days to get to know my left hand drive Mercedes. It was great to drive, having an eight speed gearbox giving a maximum of over 50mph. The powered steering was excellent and the 320hp engine pulled well. It even had an air conditioning unit on the roof, about the only thing that did not work.

I heard of a driver getting out of his cooled cab of 70°F because he had a puncture. It was 120°F outside and as he got out the heat hit him and he died of a heart attack. So I was glad it did not work.

My first driving job with White Trux was to drive to Riyadh in convoy with a colleague. First, we were to collect a load of 17mm thick steel rods from the steel storage yard on the edge of Jeddah. This was when I encountered my first problem with the Mercedes. The chassis was much higher than most trucks so I was unable to just reverse under the trailer and hook up. Even with the trailer legs wound right down I still could not get the rear of the truck to where the sloping rails helped the trailer to slide up to the 5th wheel coupling. At least the end of the chassis was under the front of the trailer, just. This would hopefully hold while I wound the trailer legs up, put some rocks under the legs and wound the legs back down to their full extent.

This was great fun on a hot day. The problem was like in the film Ice Cold in Alex, when the spring needed to be changed and the rocks slowly crumbling! Except I did not intend supporting the trailer on my back. Instead, I was hoping, "Will it hold long enough to reverse the tractor unit under the trailer?" This time it did hold, but from then on I used solid pieces of wooden blocks instead. Now I know why the other drivers did not like the Mercedes. Really hard to connect up to a trailer and the Volvos had proper sleeper cabs!

With the trailer safely on, we both drove to the steel yard to the east of Jeddah, in an industrial area. I was advised to keep my eyes peeled and drive carefully in the steel yard, as lengths of steel rod were sticking out of the sand all over the place. It would be so easy to get a puncture, and not a lot of fun changing a tyre on a very hot day.

A crane soon loaded us with well over 30 tons of steel rods, and it seemed the trailers were loaded until the double tyres were almost touching at the bottom. No weight limits in Saudi Arabia then, in fact very few rules at all. We chained the load down, and then drove back to the White Trux villa for the paperwork and a delivery address. This load was for a bridge on a new road north of Riyadh.

We left Jeddah that afternoon.

On the road at last, we were soon on the outskirts and into the open scrubland towards Mecca, 55 kilometres away. On the approach to Mecca, there is a big overhead sign advising non-Muslims to turn off to the right onto the Christian bypass. After that there were another 50 kilometres of more scrubland, the road very gradually and imperceptibly climbing all the time to reach the base of the long climb up the escarpment. From then on there is a very impressive 11 kilometre climb that is at the same gradient all the way to the top. Whoever built the road did a very good job. Nearer the top where the mountain is much steeper, so as to make the hairpin bend less sharp the road goes out on stilts (see image below). I think it was only completed in 1965, not long before that it was just a donkey trail. The many hairpins are gentle so that the two-lane highway was not only safer but we were able to stay in the same low gear all the way to the top. Going up is much safer than going down.

Many a once-loaded truck can be seen in the ravines. Some might have lost the use of the brakes from overheating or been forced off the road by careless overtaking. Trucks were not allowed to overtake anywhere on this climb, but some empty ones did, and cars were taking a chance at every opportunity.

After 40 minutes of climbing we reached the top and straight away turned right off the road onto some waste ground. There is plenty of waste ground in Saudi Arabia! The town of Ta'if was a couple of clicks down the road, but here at the top it was at least 20°F cooler with a gentle breeze. With the peace and quiet what could be better? Because of the heat haze it was impossible to see any distance, just the rugged bare rocks with the constantly busy road below twisting its way to the bottom of the escarpment.

We stayed the night in the cool air. What a difference to get a good night's sleep! We made an early start next day for the 800 kilometres to Riyadh. The road is fairly straight all the way, and as it slowly loses altitude, so it

The road winding up to Ta'if *(Courtesy of Sajith Erattupetta, Malayalam News Daily)*

gets hotter. At an average of 80kph Riyadh can be reached in 10 hours driving, stopping on the way a couple of times to get a cold Pepsi and check the tyres and load.

One thing that did surprise me on the long road to Riyadh was when the good tarmac road suddenly went from 8 metres wide like a normal road, to at least 36 metres wide. I thought it might be for turning round, or for police check points, except that they were at least three kilometres long. There were no buildings about. Just open desert. Every few hundred metres there were no parking signs, so it was not a layby. When I asked about it at our next stop I learnt that there were lots of these wider stretches of road like that all over Saudi Arabia. Apparently they were built as aircraft runways.

There were no tachographs or hours of work to worry about, just keep on going until you are tired or hungry. We both stopped for the night just before Riyadh at a roadside shack with a reed roof and dried mud walls. Outside there were a few tables with benches and wooden framework single beds with woven reeds. On the menu was our favourite, chicken and rice washed down with a cold drink.

After bypassing the main part of Riyadh City, we easily found the delivery point the next day. The tarmac road ended, waiting for a bridge to be built over a dry wadi. There were many bridges over dry wadis, because when there is the occasional heavy rain everything is awash, roads and all.

We unloaded in no time, the steel rods being dragged off the side of the trailer. On returning and going past Riyadh for 30 kilometres, my colleague pulled off the road across half a kilometre of hard desert. We were going towards a round concrete structure with a tent next to it. Inside the building was an American putting the final touches to an impressive telephone control centre. We had a chat and a meal, and pleased him no end by giving him some music cassette tapes. In exchange he gave us lots of US Army K rations. How some of them got into the country I am not sure as there was pork and beans, also tinned ham, which is all banned. The tins added an extra variety to our larder, which was more than welcome.

All around the 20' across single room were banks of exchanges with the name of a capital city above, covering the whole world.

"Do you want to call home?" the America asked. "Just dial as if you were in London."

This being the new satellite system, the line was beautifully clear. My wife thought I was in England not Saudi Arabia.

The American worker told us they were given a choice of a hotel in town or to sleep in a tent but get more money, so he chose the latter! As soon as the exchange building was built, he slept in there, and got by very well. As we were leaving he said, "Call by anytime, I am always pleased to see someone."

By that evening we were back at the same overnight parking area near Ta'if, and looking forward to the cool of the mountain top air and another good night's sleep. Next day it only took a couple of hours to get back to our base at Jeddah. That was the first trip well done.

"What's next?" I wondered.

I did three trips next, this time going north up the coast of Saudi Arabia close to the Red Sea. Each time I went to the same place, where British Steel was just starting to construct a camp. The intention to make steel eventually, I suppose, or mine the iron ore in the surrounding mountains.

On the road north, near a place called Yambu, a small sign at the side of the road read British Steel with an arrow pointing inland. A dusty track led inland, and before long there were two to three thousand foot high rugged mountains on each side. The sandy valley floor had some scrubland and the occasional tree, and was about half a kilometre wide. I managed to keep going despite some soft sand in places. The only guide was a few tracks going further up the valley. After about 10 kilometres the end of the valley came into sight with more high rocks blocking any further progress. The camp was being built entirely from scratch, with only a dozen workers there at the moment. Luckily there was a forklift on-site which made unloading the big wooden case with a generator inside a lot easier.

On the way back an artic coming in got stuck in some soft sand. With a strong chain, and engaging the three diff-locks, I was able to pull him to harder ground with no trouble. I was beginning to like this Mercedes more and more. Once back onto the tarmac road, the 300 kilometres journey south only took four hours. The nearer to Jeddah I got, the more wrecks there were

Reversed up a slope with a big crate to unload

at the side of the road until there was one every kilo-metre. Mostly cars all smashed up, but there were trucks and buses too. No parts were stripped off the wreck, as they would be in the UK. The owner, if he survived, just bought another vehicle. Accidents were "The will of Allah", which I was to hear many times.

Nearer to Jeddah there were more roadside restaurants, and also little shacks selling food. I always stopped at one particular small shack. Inside it was always dark, with rows of shelves full of household goods, plus tinned fish and fruit. Behind the small counter in the corner stood two albino men, their skin whiter than the white clothes they wore. They never went outside in the daytime, as it would be harmful to them. What I liked about them most of all was that they were always very cheerful and welcoming. It was a visit to look forward to on a hot day.

Between trips, when in Jeddah, I went to the super-market for food. It was all very expensive as everything had to be imported. My favourite place to shop was in the souk which is the market area. One street of shops was entirely given over to gold and silversmiths. Intricate brooches with very fine filigree work were sold by weight. I was invited into one goldsmiths shop by a man who spoke very good English, we had chai and talked, then I was offered one or two gold items but they were too expensive for me. I did need a gold chain for my St. Christopher and he showed me a very finely made one. I was sitting in a chair with the glass counter in front of me. I asked if it was strong, so he handed me one end of the gold chain and holding the other end, pulled me out of the chair with it so that I stood up.

"That's strong," I thought, so I bought it and still wear it today.

Another stall in the market sold cassettes of every kind of music. I liked easy listening tapes like Country, Ray Conniff, Abba and many female singers for company on the road.

One Abba double LP tape that I later took home, with many others, came out as the latest hit − two months after I had bought it! The tapes all came from Japan and, as there were no copyright laws in Saudi Arabia, were sold on the open market. I bought the tapes for the equivalent of one pound each and five or six at a time. If I did not like the tape, or it played badly, it was no trouble to change it for another one. I bought nearly a hundred tapes during the three work sessions in Saudi. The customs in England were not happy when they saw them in my suitcase.

"Where did you get these?" I was asked.

I told him I took them out with me as company when driving my truck.

"You lorry drivers are all the same, go on hop it," I was told.

"Phew, that was a bit of luck," I thought.

The next trip was to British Steel again, this time

with two forty foot trailers behind me. The front one had a 40' container full of equipment and the second an assortment of machinery. When I arrived it took longer than usual to unload as I had to drop one trailer and then hook up to the other one to reverse up the unloading ramp. I stayed the night and left next morning.

With two trailers that made it about 100' long

With two trailers near British Steel

On the way back on the tarmac road, a camel wandered into the middle of the road and stopped there. Despite having a big truck, the horn only gave a car-like "beep beep". This did not encourage the camel to move at all. Unfortunately, air horns were not allowed, unlike most countries. It was only a couple of hundred yards ahead and I had to slam on the brakes. With two trailers behind me I had thoughts of everything jack-knifing. Braking as hard as possible I looked in the mirrors but all I could see was clouds of blue smoke.

Finally, the truck came to a halt five metres from the immobile camel. Killing a camel in Saudi Arabia would cause a lot of trouble, with hefty compensation required. Not only that, hitting a camel at speed would do a great deal of damage to the front of the truck. I waited a few minutes for the smoke to clear, fearing the worst, but to my amazement the truck and trailers were in a straight line, with skid marks trailing a long way back. That pleased me even more, as driving with two trailers on always made for a more interesting drive, especially when negotiating sharp corners. Luckily, there were not many sharp bends in Saudi. I even managed to reverse the two trailers a short distance, but it was not easy.

Back safely in Jeddah I was told to take another load to British Steel, the next day. This was a large Portakabin, already loaded on a trailer. With an early start I arrived at British Steel by lunch time, and was offloaded in a couple of hours by a big crane.

On the way back through the valley I saw a big water tank over to one side, nearer the rocks. There were people next to the tank and curiosity got the better of me so I drove nearer to have a closer look. The tank was on its side, barely 5' high, 7' long and 5' deep. Living just outside sat a man and woman with four children. I said "Salaam alaykum" from a little distance away, and the man invited me over to them. A kettle was soon boiling and I was offered a glass of chai, a very refreshing drink, with no milk but I added sugar lumps. I went back to my truck for a couple of packets of biscuits and my family photos.

Any bit of shade will do

Loaded with a Portakabin

The man and woman spoke no English, but I knew a few words of Arabic and with the help of sign language and showing the photos of my wife and three children we got on very well. They had just a few possessions: some blankets, a few utensils and provisions. I had a very pleasant hour with them, and then said goodbye leaving them the biscuits. Their children were playing in the sand with small sticks and stones. No toys at all, yet they were laughing and very happy. It made me think, how little it takes to be happy in life!

Back onto the tarmac road, heading back south to Jeddah, I saw a very unusual thing. A few hundred yards to the left was a D8 bulldozer trudging across the rough desert, but with no driver? I had to stop and check. There was definitely no driver and the bulldozer was on a course to cross the road in less than a mile. I left it to it and drove on.

Twenty kilometres further down the road I saw an English truck parked on the other side of the road. I pulled across the road to park in front of him and got out to see what the trouble was. The young English driver was covered in oil and looking quite worried. He told me he had driven to Saudi Arabia from England in his old Leyland truck expecting to go home afterwards. Instead he was offered a job of delivering Portakabins for new schools to every town and village in Saudi Arabia. He was getting paid 500 pounds for each delivery, and had already made a fortune in the year of doing the job. He had a large Portakabin loaded and was en route to go to Yambu.

"Lucky fellow," I thought, until he told me why he had stopped.

The old Leyland was completely clapped out and losing power. It was belching out black smoke as it used over two litres of engine oil a day.

"What should I do?" he asked, "buy a new truck or what?"

Thinking about it, I said, "Keep running the old Leyland, as the job could stop at any time. Then when the truck finally gives up on you, leave the truck and fly home."

The oil to put into the engine was not expensive, and he thought what I told him was not a bad idea. I wished him well as I left, and told him to look out for a driverless D8 bulldozer that might be crossing the road. I hope he made his fortune; there was certainly a lot of money to be made working in Saudi Arabia. I never saw him again after that encounter.

Halfway between Yambu and Jeddah the road goes very near the Red Sea. I drove the half kilometre to get to the beach where I hoped I might be able to go for a swim. However, the sandy beach only went into a 2' deep lagoon, not quite swimming depth. I had flip flops on, anyway, which would safeguard me from getting stung by a stone fish hiding under the sand in the water. If you get stung by one of those you have less than six hours to get to a hospital before you could die! Another 30 yards out in the clear blue water, the coral started, very beautiful and very sharp. I walked carefully over the coral only to find it went into a sheer drop with no bottom in sight.

"Oh," I thought to myself, "sharks live here!"

The drop was like going over a cliff. It frightened the life out of me. So I never did get a swim in the beautiful clear warm water.

Arriving back at base in Jeddah later that evening, I was told of my next trip. There were three loaded trailers out the back, all going to the same place. I was to take one trailer and the two Volvo drivers were to take one each of the other two. Apparently, we were told by the manager, there was some desert to cross on the last stretch, so I might have to pull the other two if the going got tough. It did not sound too difficult put like that. The delivery address was Sharawrah Airport, and we were told not to tell anyone what we had loaded.

"Where's Sharawrah?" I thought.

"This could be a more interesting journey," I thought, so I got out my Bartholomew's map of the Middle East, and started looking for Sharawrah. The scale was 1 to 4,000,000 which gave 100 kilometres to the inch, so not a lot of detailed information.

I never did find any maps of just Saudi Arabia, not even in England, so I had to make do with this, the next best thing.

Going south from Jeddah

The whole journey was only nine inches on the map. Right at the bottom of Saudi Arabia, south of the Empty Quarter there was a small dot on the map with Sharawrah next to it. At least we now knew where it was, all we had to do was get there. Roughly there were 750 kilometres of tarmac road to Najran, then desert for about the last 300 kilometres.

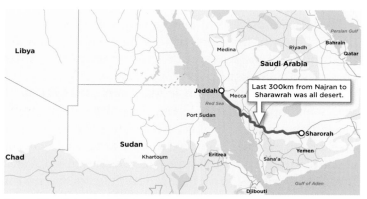

Map of Saudi Arabia, Jeddah to Sharawrah

Next morning Steve, John, and I went out to check the three loads. Whoever had loaded the trailers at the docks had done a very good job. All that was needed was to use all the straps and ropes we had to secure everything down. Each 40' trailer was evenly loaded about 8' high from the bed of the trailer. There was every shape and size of wooden crate you could think of. The only exception was a big metal fuel tank on one of the trailers. Just looking at the load gave no idea of what we were transporting, and no one would tell us what it was. We were given Saudi riyals for running money, and American dollar travel vouchers as back up as any bank would exchange them.

I had the usual trouble trying to hook up to my trailer, and after over half an hour of up, down, and up again with the legs, got my trailer safely hooked up. Steve and John were inside the villa well before I had even got the trailer on, let alone connecting up all the suzies. I checked for air leaks, and that all the lights worked. Then gave the tyres a kick to find that they were alright, and at last all was ready for the road.

I went inside, all hot and sweaty, only to find Steve and John finishing a cold drink and saying, "We've got the paperwork, are you ready to go, Gordon?"

Well, I saw no reason not to get going, so by early that afternoon we were on our way out of Jeddah. Within ten minutes we were on the outskirts of town and passing an open compound full of discarded old passenger planes, engines and wings etc. all left out in the open! In less than two hours driving, we had by-passed Mecca and climbed a thousand feet above sea level to the base of the long climb to Ta'if. It was cooler already here when we stopped to check the straps and tyres etc. Running on a flat tyre would soon cause it to overheat then catch fire. Then, in no time, the trailer and load would be going up in smoke and flames. Not good at all!

At the bottom of the climb there is a police check point and a turn off to a parking area. To avoid more of the many accidents that happened there, no trucks were allowed to use the road at night – the only night time curfew for trucks in Saudi Arabia.

On a later occasion, arriving there just before dusk, two of us from White Trux were stopped and told to park for the night in a clearing a couple of hundred yards off the road.

"It is going to be a hot sticky night," we thought.

A little while later two English trucks from another company loaded with large Portakabins pulled in and parked nearby. One of the other lads called us over and we climbed into one of the cabins on the back of his trailer. They had what looked like a plastic two litre bottle of water, but this was in fact neat alcohol, not far off a hundred per cent proof. A quarter of an inch of this in a glass topped up with Pepsi made a very strong drink. By midnight we were all well away laughing and joking. We even had a bit of a singsong!

One of the other lads who had drunk a little too much got up for a pee. He opened the cabin door and fell straight out into the pitch dark, forgetting we were six feet above the ground. We all had a good laugh, and luckily he was not hurt. We had no hangovers the next morning after a good night's sleep. Luckily the guards at the check point never heard us, or all hell would have broken loose. Drinking alcohol is a very serious offence, worse than eating pork.

This time we were well ahead of the curfew. With each trailer loaded with about seven tons of cargo, this made an all up gross weight of only 18 tons for each vehicle. So it was no hardship going up the long drag to Ta'if located at the top of the escarpment. The 11 kilometres of constant climbing took about half an hour and a few pops of the ears. Arriving at the very top, we turned sharp right onto some waste ground. We let the engines cool down, and then switched off. At first, there is a lot of heat in the cab from the engine as it is right underneath the cab. We still had enough time to go on for a couple more hours before dark, but only one of us knew the road south, so we stayed at the best place we knew. When looking over the edge of the cliff top we could see the constantly busy road twisting and turning as it zigzagged up the mountain.

If it was not for the heat haze you would be able to

see Mecca, and then Jeddah far away in the distance next to the Red Sea. As it was we were only just able to see the bottom of the cliffs. At least here it was much cooler, with a gentle breeze. This was just right for a good night's sleep. Yes, I must say it was very pleasant indeed, and there were a lot less flies too.

Because the other drivers were often away when I was at the villa or on the road I had not met Steve or John before, so now was a good opportunity to get to know each other. We talked about the work we had done before working for White Trux. Then, between us, we sorted out a meal, and had a very enjoyable evening. By ten o'clock we were in our cabs to get some sleep with the intention of getting an early start next morning.

When on the road, food-wise, fresh meat and veg-etables was never on the menu as it would not keep in the heat. I did not have room for a small fridge, so just had a store of tinned food. This consisted of corned beef, or fish like pilchards and tuna. I would eat these with biscuits if no bread was available – local bread did not keep long anyway. The PX food tins from the American working near Riyadh were also a bonus.

Going along the road there were the occasional little mud huts which were shops with a variety of tins. Out-side, a big earthenware jar about three feet high and full of water would cool the cans of Pepsi. As the water slowly evaporated through the sides of the jar it was surprising how cool this made the contents inside.

There was nothing exciting on the shelves but you could live on what was available. Nothing much in the way of a good meal to choose from, and it was more what the shop had to sell than what I really wanted. It was always too hot to want to eat much anyway. As a second course, and also as a good standby, I bought tins of fruit in juice like peaches and pears. There was plenty of room under the passenger seat to store the tins of food.

Most importantly, I always made sure I never ran out of water by taking at least double the amount I would need for a journey.

Only once in the year that I worked in Saudi Arabia did I have to worry about my supply of water. I was parked in the desert in an old petrol airport fire tender that I was to deliver to Bishah. Every fifteen kilometres it conked out with overheating, probably caused by the fuel evaporating in the carburettor. So, to help keep the engine cool, I put the heater on full. This, in theory, would add an extra means of cooling for the engine as the hot water now had an additional fan blowing through the matrix. For all the discomfort, I hoped it would help. In addition, I lifted the bonnet up which was next to me in the cab. It was like being in a blast furnace and got me an extra kilometre at most, before conking out again. I could not have got any hotter.

On one of these forced stops a Saudi in a pickup truck stopped alongside and asked for "moer", meaning water. The rule in the desert was to give half of what you had. So I gave him one of my full two litre plastic bottles of drinking water. However instead of taking a drink himself, he walked over to his pickup and gave a drink to each of the five goats he had in the back! He seemed very grateful and the goats probably were too! With a wave and "Shukran" (meaning "thank you") he was off! I was not impressed! I did not even get a glass of chai!

With all the overheating stops on that trip it took me two days to cross the 300 kilometres of desert to Bishah instead of just the one day I had hoped. The water I had left just about lasted me. In reserve, I still had two tins of peaches, which would have kept me going, in more ways than one.

It was partly my fault as I was supposed to have delivered the airport fire tender to Bishah on the back of a low loader. I knew from a previous trip just how bad the desert was going to be, so I took the fire tender off the trailer, intending to drive it there. Then I parked the truck and trailer next to a shop at the side of the road. This was where the turn off from the tarmac road went to Bishah. There were no signs or anything apart from a few tracks in the sand. I waited awhile and a big fuel tanker turned off. I waved him down and asked the driver if he was going to Bishah and could I follow him. After the first time I conked out, he just drove on leaving me to it. That was some trip, but I made it there eventually.

However, back to the present. After a good night's sleep in the cool of Ta'if, we were up early hoping to reach Najran that evening. I boiled some water on my Calor gas stove for a cup of coffee, and breakfasted on some digestive biscuits and marmalade. It was a pleasure sitting with the door open in the cool of the morning, listening to the BBC World Service on the radio and watching the sunrise. This was the best time of the day, seeing the lightening sky in the east as it extinguished the millions of bright stars in the sky. Then seeing the red orb of the sun turning bright orange as it lifted over the horizon, so that very soon it is too bright to even look at! Then the flies woke up.

By seven we were on the road driving south along the top of the escarpment. Most of the way was at 5000 feet or more, so it was never too hot, and was even at a very pleasant 80°F by midday. The excellent tarmac road gently climbed and descended with grand views of the surrounding valleys and rocky cliffs. There was very little vegetation, just the occasional bit of shrub or bush, with small trees in the dried up river beds lower down. The steep jagged crags had many cracks, showing remnants of a volcanic past. To build the road must have meant a lot of blasting. The smooth, well-built road had no steep hills or sharp bends, and very little traffic which was even better. We quite easily kept up an average of over 60kph. Being cooler and having less weight on the trailer meant there was less risk of getting a puncture.

There was only one tricky place, where the bridge over a deep ravine had not yet been built. To stop anyone driving headlong into the ravine, lots of half brick size stones were placed in the road which filtered you off to the right. Here an alternative dirt track went steeply down the 100' to the bottom with a sharp hairpin bend on the way down and another on the way up. A very shallow stream at the bottom was enough to make the first part of the climb slippery, but we all made it up. There were a couple of tangled wrecks at the bottom where the stones had not been seen by the drivers in time, most probably at night. One had landed nose first and the cab was completely squashed flat. The other wreck lay upside down, still with its load. We had some wheel spin on the loose ground on the way up, but all made it back to the tarmac road on the other side. This was a good time to check the ropes and straps on the load to see that everything was secure.

John and Steve took the lead and I trailed along behind. John had been on this road before and said there was a compound further along that we should visit. Saudi Arabia had a lot of infrastructure being built all over the country. The wealth from the oil gave them the ability to develop the country rapidly.

John pulled off the tarmac road and we followed onto a dirt track down a slope to a big walled compound. The Saudi guard opened the gates, possibly thinking we were making a delivery. We turned right and parked alongside each other, next to a big warehouse. We then followed John across the dusty 200 metres to the living quarters. We entered a larger cabin which turned out to be the restaurant, John making inquiries about his friends there. They certainly were not talking English, and looking at the notices on the wall, I saw these were all in German.

Most of the road network was being built by the Germans, with Indian and Pakistanis for the general labour. John found his friends from when he stayed over on a delivery a month before. We sat in one of the many dormitories, all having a chat for an hour. John spoke German much better than I did and they seemed to get on well. It turned out the Germans were contracted to build the missing bridge, but had been waiting nearly two months for all the equipment to arrive. So much stuff was coming into Saudi Arabia that ships were queuing up at the docks to unload.

John's friend asked if we wanted any "hooch". He took us along the corridor to a spare room where they had built a still to make their own alcohol. The end product looked just like water, but was almost 100% proof. I had heard if it was not distilled properly there was a chance of getting wood alcohol poisoning, which is quite dangerous! So we declined the offer, and said our good-byes.

Just before Abha we stopped for a cuppa, and to check the tyres and load. We pulled off the road to the right where there was a large cleared area at least a hundred metres square (see image overleaf.) We walked to the edge of the parking area and looked over the steep mountain drop to the hazy valley five thousand feet below.

The Red Sea was out there somewhere just a hundred kilometres away. I wonder if on a clear day it would be possible to see over the Red Sea, and all the way to Africa.

Three loads parked on the road to Najran

On the other side of the clearing a heavily loaded Mercedes truck was parked. The Arab driver came over and spoke to us, and at first we thought he wanted to buy whiskey as the only word we understood was whiskey. None of us had any whiskey, but then he beckoned us over to his truck and at the back of a large side locker he showed us six bottles of whiskey. Quite a lot of spirits get smuggled into Saudi Arabia despite the rigorous checks at the docks and borders. He was asking for the equivalent of £30 a bottle. Apart from this being too expensive, to get caught with whiskey or any alcohol would mean big trouble. First, there would be a spell in a very unpleasant crowded jail and then eventually a court hearing. This would be followed by a hefty fine if you were lucky, and then you would be thrown out of the country for good. So we all said, "No".

By early afternoon we had reached Abha with 400 kilometres already done that day. Here we were even higher at over 7000' and lovely and cool in the sunshine. We looked at the map and saw that we were halfway to Sharawrah already and going very well.

From Abha, the road turned east for 27 kilometres to Khamis Mushayt. The name means Thursday market – you learn something new every day! Then turning south again, still on a very good tarmac road, we left Khamis Mushayt. There was plenty of daylight left, so we decided to keep going and drive the 200 kilometres left to get us to Najran.

With only 40 kilometres to go to Najran, the road started winding gently down and down. It was getting hotter and hotter. The road levelled out at a T junction on the edge of Najran. Turning left out of the dusty town we drove along for a few kilometres and then the tarmac road just ended. That was it, one minute tarmac road, the next just sand to nowhere. Not even a stop sign! Over to the right a few tracks in the sand but no signs of any places to go to. It was worse than approaching a coastline – this was more like the end of the world as we know it.

On the left hand side, on a low hillside, there was a cluster of mud and tin buildings of a small village. On the other side was a huge palm tree plantation. This was kept watered by a truck-sized diesel engine constantly pumping water out of the ground into a big trough. From there the water was split into channels to supply the whole plantation. Little did I realize at the time how much I would rely on this nonstop supply of cool water. Here, although I did not know it at the time, was to be my base for the next two months.

We parked alongside each other near the village on an open stretch of sand. As I said before there is always plenty of waste ground in Saudi Arabia. There were no shops or a place to eat that we could see. We helped one of the Volvo drivers to unhitch his trailer and all three of us got into his cab to drive the five clicks back into Najran. All the shops were closed when we got there as it was evening prayer time and people were coming from every direction, all heading towards the mosque. Some of the latecomers were being told to hurry up by the mullahs and, in no time at all, the entire place was completely deserted. It was quite eerie in a way, with not a soul about.

However, we did not have to wait long for everybody to be back on the streets. Soon all the shutters went up and it was business as usual. We found a restaurant of sorts which had two choices of food – chicken and rice (now there's a surprise!) or kebabs. The kebabs seem to have more fat than meat, so we gave them a miss. Chicken and rice then, as the third option was to go without. We all got a smallish whole chicken and a bowl of rice, which made quite a filling meal. On the way back to the trailers we stopped outside a shop and were able to top up on a few tins of food and bottles of expensive, but vital, drinking water. It had been a long day but we had done well, and it was not long before we each went to our respective cabs to get some sleep. Here we were back down to nearly sea level and, looking at the map, less than 18° north of the Equator.

Now we were off the mountain it was well over 100°F again. Sleep was intermittent, and I was wondering what the next part of the journey would be like. Now would come the interesting bit!

Where the road ends

The next morning it was hot before we could even get started on what to do next. First was a splash and brush up in the water trough which was possibly meant for animals. It was big enough to lie in, and a lovely way to cool down. Any soapy water soon washed away into the big date plantation.

There was no chance of driving any further as there was no road, and no signs to anywhere. We did not even have a compass between us – I would have to use the sun and the stars as my compass. We had a cup of coffee and a look at the map. The next 300 kilometres as the crow flies was covered by three inches on the map. There were no road or tracks shown, just sand, a part of the Empty Quarter called Ramlet Yam, and in the tribal area of Yam as far as I could see. All these names of different areas and tribal names did not help us a lot. I was always very wary of asking for direction from an Arab. Apparently if they put their right hand out straight ahead it does not mean go straight ahead. It depends on which way the palm is facing, in this case meaning go left. So to be safe, I never asked unless they spoke English.

We were less than 20 kilometres north of the border with Yemen. In fact Najran was in Yemen until 1934, and the border as such was not very clearly marked. However, as is the case with all Bedouin tribes any borders don't mean a lot anyway.

A man approached us and, in very good English, asked us what and who we were. He told us he was Jordanian, and seemed very helpful. When we told him we were on our way to Sharawrah with these three trucks, he had a very good laugh.

"You would be lucky to get there in a 4 x 4 jeep," he said. "The only way there is going through the Empty Quarter and that has sand dunes that are up to a thousand feet high. You would have to try and stay at the top of the dunes to get along, but with the steepness of the sand there is no way you will get there in a big truck."

That cheered us up no end, so we had another cup of coffee and a think about things.

After a chat he took us to one of the bigger houses in the nearby village and spoke to an elderly man inside while we waited outside. It turned out that this man, whose name was Ali, was head of the village. Over the next two months Ali and I were to become very good friends. After greetings of "Salaam alaykum", he beckoned us all into his Toyota Crown 4 x 4 and he drove us and the Jordanian across the end of the road and onto the soft sand with tracks going all over the place. It was not possible to see where we were going as every hundred yards there was a 20' high mound of sand, held together by tufts of long grass. Driving in and out of these mounds for five kilometres or so we finally came to another small village. This one had a mosque with a minaret.

"That's my early morning call sorted then," I thought.

Apart from a couple of fairly large buildings, most of the other places were made of corrugated metal sheets. Looking at the map I think this place was called Ukhdud. There were no signs, or if there were then they were in Arabic, which was not much help to us anyway.

We were taken into a large room with beautiful Persian carpets on the floor. There were smaller ones on the wall between the windows on one side, and larger ones on the long wall on the other side; all very colourful. Sitting around the edge of the room there were about 20, mostly elderly, men dressed in brilliant white long shirts and head gear. They sat crossed-legged on cushions with their backs against the wall.

On my first trip to Doha, Qatar, in 1970 with Astran, the agent gave me a full set of Arab clothing including the head scarf and ringed headpiece. A small crocheted skull cap stopped the scarf from slipping off, even when bending down. I wished I had it to wear at this point as it was so much cooler.

A less well-dressed man came in with a tea urn and poured tea into small glass cups on a small saucer. There was no milk, which was normal, and sugar lumps to sweeten. In the glass cup there was a small spoon to stir with. Our Jordanian friend spoke to the man at the far wall, who seemed to be in charge, and then he left the room. We never saw him again after that, which was a shame.

There was a lot of tea drinking and talking which did not seem to be anything to do with our problem. After an hour we were given a lift back to our trucks by Ali, none the wiser, but the tea was good.

Leaving the trucks unguarded in Saudi was never a worry and we never even locked the doors! They had Saudi Arabia number plates so they did not look too out of place. In Saudi Arabia anyone who is caught stealing lives in dread of having their right hand chopped off. This is the only hand you are allowed to eat with, so stealing was unheard of.

How we were going to continue this delivery was proving to be not just hard but at the moment it looked unachievable. With the short journey to Ukhdud being all soft sand, it would be impossible for the two Volvos to get over the first 50 yards of soft sand without grinding to a halt. With the thought of 300 kilometres of desert to cross, there was no way I wanted to have to tow them one at a time on the difficult bits, especially when a difficult bit was less than 50 yards away from the start!

There were no phones or any other way to get in touch with our base at Jeddah, so, after a lot of deliberating, I decided Steve and John should leave their trailers with me and head back to Jeddah. They could tell the manager the problem with the last 300 kilometres to Sharawrah, and that I would have to try to sort out a way of getting there myself. No one ever came down from Jedda to see how I was getting on, so I suppose I made the right decision. Meanwhile, Steve and John could earn more money on the more normal work.

When I usually had a problem with paperwork at border crossings on Middle East work I always asked to see the man at the top. Going to the Director of Customs with the words "Can you help me please?" seemed to work wonders. So I went to see the head man in the village and, with my limited Arabic, explained I needed to drive my truck to Sharawrah.

This time in the Toyota 4 x 4 we went into Najran and to the prince's palace. I was introduced to the prince and asked to sit down on one of the cushions in a room with lovely coloured rugs on the floor and walls. Like all Arabs the men were wearing long shirts down to their ankles and everyone had a headscarf. I noticed that not all the men in the room had white headscarves, which is the norm in places like Jeddah. Down here in Najran there were many with red and white chequered scarves. Maybe it meant a different tribe or area. In a hot country like Saudi Arabia it was the perfect clothing. The white shirt kept the sun off, and the headscarf was very useful in a sand storm, as well as being cooler. All the shirts were brilliant white but somehow the prince's shirt was even brighter. He looked very imposing, with a gold braid around the collar and a triple cord over his headdress. At a guess, the prince was about 50 years old, unlike all the other Arabs in the room who were much older. They did not look like relatives, so maybe they were just advisers. It seemed that any distant relative of the crown prince was made a prince in Saudi Arabia. So I sat cross-legged for ages until a man who spoke French came in. At least my French was a little better than my Arabic. I explained about the three trailers that needed to go to Sharawrah Airport, and asked if I could get help in finding a way to get there.

"This will take time to arrange, and you will need a letter of authority," I was told. I was ushered out of the room. There seemed little hope of getting something sorted out quickly. I went back to my truck with Ali. On the way we stopped at a shop and Ali bought a six pack of bottled non-alcoholic beer. He parked on the edge of town and we quietly drank two cans each.

It seemed I was completely in the hands of the local people to get me any further. While I waited I took all the ropes and straps off the two trailers that would be staying behind and used everything I had to secure the load down on my trailer. One way or another I was determined to get the job done.

Next morning the head man took me across the soft sand to the small village of Ukhdud in his Toyota 4 x 4, and again we were seated in the large room with about 20 elders and we drank more chai.

By watching the other people in the room, I soon learnt that if you put your empty glass down it was soon filled with chai again, but I also noticed that those that did not want any more turned their glass upside down on the saucer. Then again, if you needed more chai you held the saucer with the little finger and rattled the glass in the saucer when the chai man approached you. Even when one was drinking, the spoon stayed in the glass, so I had to be careful when taking a sip to keep the spoon to the side of my nose, and not up it! At least it was too short to poke you in the eye! I already knew that you should never show the soles of your shoes or feet towards anyone in the room. Apparently this is an insult so one sat crossed-legged all the time. There were lots of customs to learn, but then, "when in Rome do as the Romans do" was my motto. There was a lot of talking, but whether it was dealing with me I never found out.

Shortly after midday everyone left, and I was given a lift back to the village across the soft sand. With each journey it did not seem so formidable to and from Ukhdud, so that in a couple of days I could find my own way there with just the Mercedes unit. Later that afternoon the head man, Ali, invited me to a trip into Najran. Not in his new Toyota Crown, but in a beaten up old Dodge pickup. It had a comfortable bench seat and much softer suspension, and I think Ali preferred it. As it had only two wheel drive it was only useful on the tarmac roads. We stopped outside a shop and he bought another six bottles of non-alcoholic beer. It tasted a bit like beer, a pity it was not cold, and at least it was legal to drink! It was the nearest you could get to going down the pub for a drink. We did this every afternoon. I think he liked to show me off to the people of Najran, either that or I made a good excuse to buy some beer!

The next day being Friday, as on our Sunday, nothing happened. The previous two days were not much better and I soon learnt the word bukra, meaning tomorrow. It just showed the difference in attitude between say a Londoner and an Arab here. In the city everything must be done right away or even before. To an Arab there is always tomorrow so why rush. Also, being told bukra keeps you happy, even if they know it will take days longer.

When told bukra you think, "Well, tomorrow is not too bad I suppose." However, it is rarely tomorrow or even the day after that.

The pace of life had slowed right down here and I realized I would have to get used to it. In town there were no phones, or a post office to send a telegram, so I just had to sit and wait, and hope for the best.

On the fifth day, Ali took me to the prince's palace again. The palace was not like a palace with shining domes and mosaics on all the outside walls. Inside there were just bare plaster walls in all the dozen or so rooms and they were all on one level. Most of the rooms were for sleeping. It was all very basic, with just a single bed and a chair.

Ali and I were ushered through to the prince's more luxurious room, where we squatted down and waited. After a while two burly Bedouins, each with crossed bandoliers and an old Lee Enfield rifle, came into the room. Unlike all the other Arabs who were dressed in white, of these two rough looking Bedouins one had a greenish shirt with red and white headgear while the other had a brown shirt and no headgear at all, which was unusual. These two, I was told, were to be my guides to Sharawrah.

Next, I was given a letter all in Arabic which was to give me the authority to go to Sharawrah. I was so pleased; at last real progress!

Thanking the prince with a big grin and saying "Shukran" (meaning "thank you") a few times, I shook hands with the formidable looking Bedouins and everyone else in the room. When asking when we would be leaving, I was told bukra. On the way back to my truck I was thinking, "Things are looking up!" The next part of the journey was looking a reality at last.

That afternoon I drove the Mercedes and loaded trailer to the small village of Ukhdud. Despite the soft sand, the going was level and, in 15 minutes, I was parked on the edge of the village near the big room. There was a place to eat which was good, but nowhere to wash which was bad!

Ukhdud village, with my truck in the foreground

The next day, in the morning, I was beckoned into the large room with the elders. My letter of authority was passed round and, with lots of nodding of heads, it was then given back to me. We all had lots of tea, and everyone seemed to take turns in saying something. After the meeting, the two Bedouins came to the truck and I thought we were set to move off, but it was not to be! They said, "Bukra" – yet another delay!

Just after midday the next day, a Toyota Crown 4 x 4 pulled up next to my truck and a young boy of about 14 got out of the driver's seat. He had two friends or slightly younger brothers with him, and I could tell by how smartly they were dressed they came from a well-to-do family. They beckoned me into their Toyota and we went just a hundred yards to stop outside the restaurant.

The eldest ordered a big metal bowl of rice covered in a cloth, four cooked chickens and half a dozen bottles of water. Together with plates and cutlery we put it all in the vehicle and without paying as far I could see, off we went again. Maybe the food was ordered earlier, as I doubt there were such things as "put it on the account". More and more I got the impression this boy was the son of a prince. He was a good driver, and had no trouble driving on the soft sand and out past the outskirts of the village.

Threading our way through more and more rocky outcrops, we went round a bend and saw an amazing sight. Just ahead was a massive rock suspended above the sand upon three huge smooth rounded rocks (see overleaf.) A blanket was put on the sand under this rock, and that was where we were to eat our meal. Well, I never expected this to happen, life is full of surprises. Because the sun never shone under the rock it was that little bit cooler. A full bottle of water was used to wash the clean plates and cutlery, and tissues were used to wipe them dry.

The enormous rock just five feet above us must have weighed 50 or even 100 tons.

I thought to myself, "Well, it's been there many years, so another couple of hours should be alright."

We each had a whole small chicken and spooned some tasty fluffy white rice onto our plates. The boys laughed and giggled a lot of the time and, not knowing what the joke was myself, I laughed with them. The eldest boy knew a few words of English, but not enough to have a conversation. I was picking up Arabic words all the time. Learning the numbers I found was very useful. Towards the end of the meal I got hold of

Huge rock on three supports where we sat and had chicken and rice with young boys.

a wish bone and showed them how you pull it apart with the little finger. I tried to explain about making a wish but trying to explain that was beyond me. So I just patted the one that ended up with the biggest piece on the back. We all had a good time, and before long I was taken back to the village.

If we really were going to start the next day I thought I had better check the engine oil and water levels again to be sure I was ready. The ropes and straps were all tight, so there was nothing else to do but wait.

That night it was very hot again. On one side of me there was a high mass of rocks, and on the other the village, so no breeze could get through. I kept wondering if we would really be going tomorrow, or would it be bukra again.

Across the desert to Sharawrah

Six days after arriving at Najran there were signs of progress at last. The two Bedouins arrived earlier than expected in the morning driving a 4 x 4 Toyota Crown. I had just made myself a mug of coffee, and a snack to eat for breakfast, when they pulled up alongside my cab. With loud shouts of "Yalla, yalla" and an arm beckoning to me, they moved off obviously expecting me to follow. The coffee went out the window, there was no time to warm the engine up as I liked to, and off we started. Luckily the air pressure was up just enough to get moving.

Well, at last we were on the move, but what would happen next was still a mystery for the moment. To the south of the village there extended a 10 metres high embankment of rocks, and then sand. Driving along the base of this we came across a narrow gap cut through the sand dune, and out into the empty desert beyond. I had no idea how the journey would be from here on, and did not relish trying to climb steep mountains of sand. There had been a week of next to nothing happening, or so it seemed, and now it was all rush, rush, rush. My plate of breakfast fell off the seat onto the cab floor, so I was not even able to have my "meals on wheels"!

The desert was fairly hard and level to start with.

"If only it stays like this," I thought.

Where the wind had constantly blown the loose sand away this left a really hard surface, but this did not last for long, unfortunately. As the sand got increasingly soft and the wheels dug in, so the engine started to labour. Even with my foot hard on the accelerator my speed got slower and slower. Changing down another gear I managed to keep up momentum, but only just. The Toyota, meanwhile, started to pull away and leave me far behind.

"When will they notice I am not behind them?" I thought to myself. I don't think mirrors get used very much in the desert! I had only gone 50 kilometres and was losing my guide already. Thinking about it I realized I had not offered to pay anyone, maybe they thought I was not worth it!

With no sign of the sand changing back to the harder surface, now was the time to use the diff-locks. The three square push-on switches on the dash each had a slightly different symbol on them. They all showed the outline of a 6 x 6 vehicle. The first one showed a cross in the middle of the two axles at the back of my unit; this locked the two rear differentials. The second had a cross on the front axle which locked the front steering axle differential. The third had a cross in a small square in the middle of my truck which locked the transfer box. This last one locked the front and rear wheels all together so that all six wheels would go round at the same speed. Without the diff-locks, it only needed one wheel to start spinning and the vehicle would come to a standstill. With all diff-locks engaged this gave me much better traction, and I was able to keep going, but I was down to only 20kph. My guides had now disappeared into the distance. All I had was the tracks of their Toyota to follow. With my fingers crossed I followed them. It was hot enough without sweating about getting lost or stuck completely.

The desert stretched for miles ahead and on either side. There were no features with which to get a bearing. The sun was almost directly overhead now, so I did not know if I was going east or south. There was just no way of telling! If only I had a compass! Ahead there was another change in the colour of the sand, and I was back onto firmer ground. I disconnected the diff-locks so as not to put any stress on the transmission. Then I was able to pick up speed again to a steady 60kph. In the distance I could make out a pile of rocks. It was impossible to tell how far away they were because of the heat haze and shimmering air. As I followed the Toyota tracks, I got nearer to the rocks, and there was the Toyota parked with the bonnet up. I hoped this was to help cool the engine, and not that it had a problem.

What a relief it was to catch up to my guides, I was sweating enough with the heat, let alone the thought of being marooned. The hot air was not only uncomfortable it seemed to befuddle my mind, so that even thinking sensibly was not easy.

I was totally reliant on my Bedouin guides. While chasing after them I had begun to realize how big and empty this desert journey was becoming. All I knew was that Sharawrah was somewhere to the west and still over 200 kilometres away. Suppose I was left alone and then the truck broke down? I only had ten two-litre bottles of drinking water, which at the most would last me about two or three days. I wondered what the chances of being rescued out here were. There were only two people who knew roughly where I was. This could be a more daunting journey than I thought.

I stopped near to the rocks. Strange that a hundred feet high mound of rocks should just be jutting out of the sand! With the sun directly overhead there was no shade anywhere except under the trailer, but the sand was too hot even for that. I did not risk sleeping on the sand like I saw the Bedouins doing. There are scorpions and snakes that are all poisonous. So while the Bedouins slept I made myself a snack of

My Bedouin guides

pilchards and cream crackers. It made a change from chicken and rice!

I got to thinking that whilst I had enough drinking water for a couple of days or so, I had nothing for the truck if there was a water leak.

"I will worry about that when it happens," I thought. I still did not know how long it would take to go the 300 kilometres to Sharawrah.

While waiting for the Bedouins to wake up I climbed to the top of the rocks. Half way up I had a scare when an owl flew out in front of me, and made me nearly lose my footing. This got me thinking about being more careful. At the top of the rocks I could see for miles in all directions. In the distance, roughly in the same direction we were travelling, there was another outcrop of rock. To the north I could just see a steep ridge of sand hundreds of feet high – this must be the Empty Quarter I guessed. On climbing carefully back down to my truck, I used my note book to draw the shape of the rocks. It was basically just a pyramid with nothing to make it outstanding, but at least it was a land mark.

"I must remember to make a note of the distances and any other observations," I thought. "If only I had a compass to check on which direction we were heading!"

With the sun now directly overhead it was impossible to tell which way was which. There were no trees here to check which side the moss was growing. When the sun got a bit lower in the sky I could use my watch to find north. This was a trick I learnt in the Boy Scouts! Say it is about four o'clock, assume it is exactly on the hour with the minute hand and point your watch with the sun half way at two o'clock. If you draw an imaginary line from twelve to six o'clock, and north is where the six is pointing. Just like that!

At about two o'clock we were on the move again, and I was glad the hard sand continued. It was soon possible to see the next stack of rocks and we passed by fairly close, but this time we did not stop. These rocks where about the same shape and size as the last lot, and there were 35 kilometres between them. I made a note of that. Still on hard sand, 20 kilometres later up ahead in the distance I could see a small tree. I did not give it much thought as there were miles of open desert in every direction. Driving at 60kph the tree came up more quickly than I would have thought and I nearly drove into it. I resolved to be more careful in future. Maybe the shimmering heat was getting to me! Luckily I was wearing good sunglasses.

We travelled more south than east for the next 30 kilometres. I did not give a thought as to whether or not we were still in Saudi Arabia, I just assumed we were. Even the map I had did not show where Saudi Arabia and Yemen had their border. The hard sand was still mainly level to begin with, then slightly softer sand again with a few undulations.

The Toyota disappeared over a rise and, as I followed, "Wow!" I exclaimed. There was a small village! It was more a cluster of colourful tents, no more than a dozen altogether. I stopped a couple of hundred metres away from the nearest tent.

Quite often when I stop, every child in the vicinity comes to stare at me, but this time nobody came – maybe there were no children. In front of me there was a well, without it I doubt if anyone would be camping here. Over the well there was a long tapering wooden pole held eight feet up by two uprights. On the shorter, thicker end a net full of rocks helped to counterbalance the longer end which had a bucket on a rope to go in the well.

While I waited, a pickup truck stopped by the well and two Arabs started to fill a truck sized inner tube. It had been cut in half like a crescent moon, and the ends sealed up except for an opening to fill up with water. It seems anything that can hold water is of value in the desert.

I'm sure if you offered an Arab a choice of a half-litre gold flask or a two-litre plastic bottle, the plastic bottle would be chosen every time as it holds more water.

None of my load was of any use to anyone, but in the desert different things have different uses. The crates would make a lot of firewood, and any small container could be used to hold water. It was the first time I had thoughts of something going missing. Out here in the equivalent of the wilderness I had the impression that it was completely lawless, yet I always felt safe enough.

For some reason I did not fancy having a walk round the village of tents, which was unlike me, as I always wanted to see everything. The inhabitants looked a pretty rough lot. They were true travellers of the desert, staying here for a few days then moving on. I stayed in the cab after checking round the vehicle. The back of the trailer was covered in sand dust, the load was secure and there were no leaks from the engine. So far, so good. I tried to get some sleep but it was much too hot, and there were always a couple of flies for company. Slowly the sun went down and still nothing happened, no one came to see me. Without being told anything, I assumed I was here for the night. It was too late now to get going anyway.

Even after dark it was too hot to sleep, so I sat on top of the trailer load looking at the stars. The Milky Way seemed to light up the whole sky and the millions of stars seemed close enough to reach up and touch. When driving on the Middle East run with Astran and going through Eastern Turkey the road was mostly at five to six thousand feet up. The night air was clear, just as it was here. In the summer I slept on the roof of the trailer, stargazing before going to sleep. I had a book by Patrick Moore called Naked Eye Astronomy. It explained the constellations and what main stars are visible each month. I learned the names of the main stars, and all the constellations, and, of course, how to find the North Star. This was to prove very useful on the forthcoming trips.

I never trusted water from wells, only that in plastic bottles from shops, but on this occasion, as I had a couple of empty plastic bottles I filled them up at the well and kept them to one side for emergencies. To avoid dehydration I drank six or seven litres of water a day.

It was difficult to get to sleep at first, but gradually the air cooled as it does every night, and in the early hours it was cool enough to need a blanket.

The next day, by mid-morning, my two Bedouin guides arrived in their Toyota, but then they turned round and drove off again back among the tents without a word. Half an hour later they were back, this time in a brand new Toyota 4 x 4.

"How did they do that?" I wondered.

At last we got going again, this time more to the east, on a mixture of mostly good or not too soft sand. As I followed the Toyota, keeping out of the dust it threw up, it suddenly swerved off to the left. I thought they were avoiding some soft sand, but it looked alright as I turned after them. A small dark shimmering dot in the distance gradually turned out to be a Bedouin encampment. There were a dozen camels grazing nearby on what little bits of scrub they could find. My Bedouins parked 50 metres away and slowly walked to the opening that was in the middle of a tent. When they were about three or four metres away, they stopped, squatted down and waited. A few minutes later they were beckoned inside. I was parked a bit further away and sat in the cab and waited, and waited (see image overleaf.) To pass some time I walked round the truck to check that the load was secure and that there were no flat tyres. All was well, so I sat in the cab again. Half an hour dragged by until I got tired of waiting.

Because of the heat, I wore only shorts and flip flops or boots depending on where I was. I put a shirt on and walked over to the tent and waited outside as I had seen my two Bedouins do. After a while, I was beckoned in by the two Bedouins from the tent. They wore very colourful robes, and I was invited to squat on a beautiful rug. All around there were multi-coloured cushions scattered about to lean on.

Parked in front of a Bedouin camp

I was offered an ornate cup of green coffee poured out of a brass jug with stiff camel hairs to hold the beans back. The decorated china cups were all filled, and it felt like a very relaxing atmosphere. I added sugar lumps to my coffee to make it a bit more palatable as it was very bitter. All the chinaware was transported in brass containers which were put to one side. On either side of me, an area was partitioned off which must have been the sleeping area. Inside it did seem a bit cooler. I heard the tents were made of goat hair, and although it was hot outside that made it cooler inside. It was all very luxurious and comfortable and I really admired their way of life.

After the coffee I was handed a metal bowl containing frothy camel's milk, I guessed. I dislike any milk, and this was even worse to me. I took a small sip to be polite, hoping not to be offered any more. The four Bedouins chatted for an hour, and then we all shook hands and said our goodbyes. This was an interesting look at how the nomads of the desert lived.

The more I drove on the desert, the more I was learning about it all the time. I soon learnt to check the tracks I was leaving in the sand before stopping. If it was too deep it was not safe to stop, as once stationary getting moving again could be a problem. Depending on the winds it could be soft for a 100 metres then harder again. To hear the engine straining soon told you when the sand was softer.

In the morning and afternoon the shadows from the sun gave a better idea of the undulations in the sand dunes. Towards midday it was difficult to see any dips. To hit one of those at speed could be disastrous. On the hard level stretches it was so easy to become complacent. With no feature in the distance to focus on, the sand would apparently roll away underneath, but you seemed to be still in the same place.

On one such hard surface I noticed ahead a slight change in the colour of the sand. I was ahead of the Toyota, doing 60kph and not taking a lot of notice when, to my horror, the sand dropped away down a long steep 45° slope. I slammed the brakes on but it seemed I was destined to drop over the edge.

The sand did not offer much grip compared to a tarmac road, but luckily just before the razor sharp drop off, the sand became softer and the wheels started to dig in. I finally stopped with the front wheels right on the edge. To have gone over at any sort of speed down the 300 metre drop would have needed a miracle to survive. Any deviation to one side or the other and the whole lot would have rolled over and over to the bottom, becoming a complete wreck and with me in it! Unless I was able to jump out!

For a few moments I just stayed still and slowly calmed down. It is surprising just how steep a slope of sand can be when carved out by the wind. As the wind eats away at the hard packed sand it is reluctant to slide down. I was so near the edge it was not even safe to get out of the cab.

So first I had to stop and think, "How do I get out of this without making it worse?" Just as I was beginning to feel a little calmer, the front wheel on my side lurched and started sinking. The sand at the edge had started giving way, slowly tilting the cab. An avalanche of sand was sliding down the slope, getting bigger as it descended.

"All will be lost if I don't move away quickly," I thought. "The whole truck and trailer will start to go over the edge." I tried to avoid panic mode!

First I engaged the three diff-locks, carefully selected reverse gear, and without too many revs, waited to see what would happen as I eased the clutch up. Reverse is a very low gear and even though the wheels dug in she slowly managed to edge away from the drop, and back onto the harder sand. To say I was relieved is an understatement.

Another lesson learnt – I must keep a look out for the slightest change in the colour of the sand. We continued by going along the top then down a much smaller sand dune. By keeping in a generally east direction, we were making good time. After that there were no outcrops of rock, just nothing in all directions. It was completely flat and lifeless. For the whole of the journey I never saw another vehicle and no other tracks in the sand.

Just before a slight rise in the sand ahead, the Toyota stopped and the Bedouins got out of their 4 x 4. I, too, got out to stretch my legs and was cautioned to be quiet. The Bedouins slowly eased their way carefully near to the top and laid down crawling forward to look over the edge. I went back to my cab and brought back to them my pair of 7 x 50 binoculars. They were very impressed with these and spent some time checking this huge flat area in front of us, into which you could have fitted the whole of London. Instead, there was absolutely nothing except for a couple of sand devils, small whirlwinds, dancing round each other as they slowly drifted across the wide plateau. My Bedouins seemed satisfied with what they saw, or did not see, and after a while we pressed on. We were able to go at a good speed for the next 30 kilometres over this flat empty bowl. Here it seemed even hotter.

Soon the small sand dunes started again and the going got much softer. Even with the diff-locks engaged I came to a halt. I tried to reverse and get a run but only achieved an extra metre. With the help of the two Bedouins, we let the truck tyres down to about 60 pounds per square inch. This gave the tyres a bigger profile, and much more grip. It was enough to get moving me again. Another lesson learned! Now I would have to be careful not to do any sudden turns as this could pull the tyres off their rims. As soon as the surface got hard again I disengaged the diff-locks. The tyres looked safe enough at the lower pressure so I left them as they were. On the last 70 kilometres to Sharawrah the sand turned to gravel in places and we made good progress. The Bedouins certainly knew their way. I would never have managed this on my own, even with a compass! And I certainly could not have done it with the other two drivers and their Volvo trucks.

Before long the landscape changed. At first all I could see was the top of a gantry as the gravel and stones went up and down on long waves. Then I could see more buildings, and the town of Sharawrah came into view. The two Bedouins drove off and I never saw them again!

It was quite late in the day, so I parked near a fence which I assumed was the airfield. I was too tired to look around, so had a bite to eat in the cab, and completed my notes on the journey.

"So this is Sharawrah," I thought. There did not seem to be a lot here, but at least I was very pleased to have arrived safely.

Next morning I found the gate leading into what turned out to be a military-only airfield. A guard on the gate kept me waiting while his colleague went off and eventually came back with an officer. I showed him the paperwork, but would not let him keep it explaining that there were three trailers altogether. He spoke a fair amount of English, enough to understand what I was trying to do. Once inside the gate, the next question was where do I unload and how? I was hoping for a warehouse with a big forklift. The officer told me the load could not go into the spare hanger as the flight commander kept his goats in there! He found an empty space inside the fence and said I was to unload it all there out in the open. I took off all the ropes and straps and waited.

It was a strange airport as there was not one plane in sight, and none were landing or taking off. After another hour, a large earth mover with a three metre wide bucket on the front turned up. It had bigger tyres than my truck, so had no trouble on the soft sand. Considering the lack of communication with the driver we made a good team. With the aid of a strap we took one crate off at a time. Most fitted in the bucket, but the extra-large ones needed to be held on with a strap wrapped around the case and onto the bucket.

The driver wasn't so careful unloading the crates to the ground, tipping the bucket forward when it was still at least a metre in the air. Three hours later everything was unloaded, with all the crates scattered about on the sand – what a mess! No one came to check what I had delivered or to supervise the unloading.

The last thing to be done was to lift my spare tyre onto the trailer and strap it down. There was nowhere on the truck to stow a big tyre so it always got moved about a lot. It was just the tyre and had no metal wheel on it – this made it much lighter to move, and I had all the equipment I needed to change tyres.

Because of the extra drag of driving on sand, and often driving in low gears, my fuel was down to half. This was not enough to safely get back safely to Najran. There were only a few dusty roads in the town, with no tarmac roads at all and, as far as I could see, no garages to fill up at. I drove back to the airfield and eventually found the same officer. He was not happy when I explained I needed fuel to get back to Najran.

After a lot of talking with another officer, I was re-luctantly given 200 litres of diesel on the promise that on the next journey I would replace the 200 litres loaned to me. I offered to pay, but that was declined. I asked about where I could find the Bedouins who brought me here.

"Where is your letter of authority?" I was asked.

I showed the officer the letter I had been given by the prince in Najran. He read it and told me that this letter was for me to go from Najran to Sharawrah, it said nothing about going back to Najran again. I could not believe it!

"With two more trailers still to get here, now what do I do?" I thought.

Not getting any easier

I left my truck parked on the outside of the perimeter fence near the main gate, then made my way across the sand for a couple of hundred metres to walk into Sharawrah. There were no tarmac roads, just sandy roadways, with the occasional narrow alleyway. There were no front gardens and houses, as in England. Instead there was a high wall, over two metres high, with closed metal gates. With nobody about to ask about finding the head man or the prince if there was one, I was not having much luck. I would need someone to guide me back to Najran!

The small town of Sharawrah had two parallel roads one way, and two at right angles the other way, just like a noughts and crosses game. A bit further away from the town, to the south, was a tall girder framework with a corrugated housing on top, and what looked like a conveyer going up to it. It was all unused and derelict, but must have been the means to make the hardcore or tarmac for the runway. Seeing this structure on a following trip was to possibly save my life!

With only a hundred metres between each crossroads, I had toured the whole place in 10 minutes, and met nobody. On one corner I saw a door open and went over to investigate. The writing on the wall said Saudi Bank in English and Arabic. With one foot over the doorstep, I was immediately stopped from going any further by a man blocking my way. The floor of the five metre square room was completely covered with stacks of Saudi riyal notes. The two bankers inside must have just finished counting all the regular piles of money, and did not seem bothered by me watching them. In the corner was a free-standing, two metre high metal safe with the door open.

What happened next surprised even me, and I thought I had seen some strange things in my travels. The man nearest me got a broom, and began to sweep all the money back into the safe.

"That's one way to do it!" I thought.

After the money was all swept in I was allowed to enter. I was pleased that the banker behind the counter spoke some English. I told him I had driven to Sharawrah from Najran by truck and needed to get back again. On asking about a prince or head man, I was told that neither lived in Sharawrah.

This was a blow and put me back to square one! Feeling at a loss, I walked back to my truck to make myself a refreshing cup of tea and have a think. Nobody seemed in the slightest bit concerned to help me – if anything I was a nuisance and best left alone. Then as if in answer to a prayer, help came from quite an unexpected direction!

It was four o'clock, the hottest time of day, when normally there was nobody about. I was just thinking of going into the airport to see the flight officer again, when a cloud of dust followed the arrival of six big Army tank transporters.

They all stopped a couple of hundred yards away on the edge of town. I walked over to take a look and for something to do. An officer got out of the 4 x 4 jeep that had been in the lead, and I went up to him to say "Salaam alaykum". Luckily he spoke a little English, so I explained I had come from Najran and wanted to get back there again.

"We are going to Najran in the morning," he said. I asked if I could go with them. Well, he did not say "yes" but then he did not say "no", it was more like a maybe. "Joy of joys," I thought, at last a safe way out of this dusty unhelpful place.

I had two more journeys back here still to do. What a game this was turning out to be! At least I knew now what I was in for, or so I thought!

It was best not to think about any more problems at the moment. The first thing was to get back to Najran. When I am alone my mind sometimes goes through all that can go wrong, then if it happens at least I am prepared. The trouble is, what goes wrong is often the unexpected, so it is back to the drawing board!

To make sure I would not be left behind in the morning, I moved my truck and parked it next to one of the huge tank transporters. None of the big articulated low-loaders had a tank loaded on the back, which was just as well, as they would have got stuck a lot more often in the soft sand. I thought my truck looked big, but parked next to one of the Army trucks with their huge, wide sand tyres, this made mine look like a baby.

My Merc next to an Army low-loader

I am not very good at getting up early in the morning anywhere, but especially in Saudi Arabia. At night I slept relatively mosquito-free in the cab. Even at

11 p.m. it was still over 100°F inside and out. Then by two or three in the morning it started to get much cooler and instead of tossing and turning with the heat, I needed to grab a blanket. From then on I could get some proper sleep for a few hours.

On this morning, it seemed, I had only just got to sleep when all hell broke loose. The transporter next to me had started his engine, giving it a few loud revs of the big engine. As I looked out the window, all bleary eyed, he was driving off following the others. Panic stations! The sun was not even up and I certainly wasn't up. I quickly got dressed, which meant putting on my shorts. Right, what to do next? I must try to get my brain in gear.

On a normal day I would have put the kettle on, have a splash of water over my face and clean my teeth. Then I would sit with a cup of black coffee and biscuits for at least half an hour as I woke up slowly. I'm not good first thing; in fact, I feel worse in the morning than when I go to bed.

As I started the engine, looking out of the window all I could see was the cloud of dust trailing off into the distance. I had no time to check the oil, water or tyres. It has been known for people to sleep under vehicles, so it was always best to check before moving off, but not today.

After starting the Mercedes engine, I then had to wait for the air warning buzzer to stop. When that stopped it meant there was enough air pressure built up in the air tanks to release the hand brake. It is a fail-safe system that if the air pressure is not above about 70 pounds per square inch then even if the handbrake is released the truck brakes would still stay on.

When one is driving along, if there is a bad air leak, as when say the trailer separates from the truck, this rips all the airlines and the brakes will automatically come on. It happened to me once in Yugoslavia when the trailer "A" frame broke. My trailer careered across the road and the brakes automatically came on and it stopped just before going into a ditch and possibly turning over.

As always when starting the cold engine first thing in the morning, I never liked to rev the engine too much. My motto was "look after the engine and the engine will look after you". It seemed to take much longer than usual for the air to build up. It's always the same when you are in a hurry! At last, the buzzer stopped and I was able to get going and chase after the army trucks, which were now just a cloud of dust fading into the distance.

To watch the sun come up to a new day was always impressive in the desert. It's moments like this that make up for all the other discomforts, but not today! I splashed my face with water to get some of the sleep out of my eyes. There was no sign of the convoy anywhere out in the distance, but at least the tyre tracks were unmistakable, and I used them to show me where they had gone. With the engine soon warmed up, I started to put my foot down and pick up speed.

For two hours I did not seem to be getting any closer to the convoy as they were obviously not hanging about. The surface, to start with, was mostly small stones with some bigger ones to go round. It was very noisy, unlike the sand which is more a swishing sound, barely audible over the sound of the engine. The stony surface gave less chance of getting stuck, but more chance of getting a puncture. The stones and gravel soon changed to sand and this was getting a little softer with every kilometre.

Then the two shimmering dots in the distance finally turned out to be two stationary transporters. One was definitely stuck with its drive wheels buried over a foot deep in the sand. The driver had made the mistake of driving in another vehicle's tracks. One trick I soon learnt driving in the desert was to always drive on unused sand. The wind and the change in day and night temperature leaves a thin hard crust, just enough to give extra support to drive on, but only the once.

The Army drivers did not seem to be very experienced at desert driving. This driver was only digging in deeper with his drive wheels spinning in an effort to get going. I stayed a couple of hundred metres away to watch the fun. The transporter driver did not even try making a rut by going backwards and forwards, he just went forwards, digging in deeper. The second transporter got in front and, by using the winch on his trailer, secured the cable to the stranded truck. With lots of black smoke and revving engines the front one pulled away. The winch brake had not been applied and the cable was extended by 50 metres! The stuck transporter did not move at all. I never ceased to be amazed in the Middle East, and I had to laugh. With the winch brake applied another attempt was made and, with more revving and black smoke, and with the wheels spinning, the stranded truck was heaved out of its hole and able to get going on its own again.

My truck tyres still had about 60 pounds per square inch and were coping very well. This was not low enough to do any damage, but enough to give that extra traction needed at times. I went round the patch of softer sand now scarred with deep ruts, and followed the last two transporters. I was keeping a look out for the other tracks all the time. At the moment it was easy to see the fresh tracks of the other vehicles, but within a few days, with the first breath of wind, these would probably fade away.

Ahead, the horizon shimmered in the heat haze, level and featureless. The only guide of sorts was the towering sand hills of the Empty Quarter to the north. The softer sand only slowed us down, but no one got stuck again. For a while there were low sand dunes to go over, but any speed lost going up was soon gained when going down the other side.

We caught up with the other four transporters and the 4 x 4 at a rock outcrop, just like the one we saw on the way out. All the transporters were parked at different angles all over the place, not very Army-like, but I

Parked Army low-loaders with drivers

Looking down from the top of the rock outcrop

expect none of them wanted to stop unless they could park where the sand was hard.

I tried to make friends with the other drivers, but they did not seem interested in me, and they were soon all grouped together for midday prayers. I always wondered how they know which way it was to Mecca: maybe it was just guesswork. I kept a little to one side, drank my long awaited morning coffee, and kept an eye open for any signs of getting on the move again.

My fuel gauge was reading just over a quarter. It was not a good idea to let it get any lower, as when the fuel gets low in the tank there was more chance for the sediment on the bottom to get stirred up. It can then clog up the filters and maybe even the fuel pump and engine. The fuel from the filling stations in Saudi Arabia was not as clean and well filtered as back home. The change in temperature from day to night changes the air pressure in the vehicle's fuel tank, and this also lets in the finest of dust.

I once saw a brand new fridge that was being unwrapped from its polystyrene cover. When the fridge door was opened inside there was a fine layer of dust!

Condensation can also build up with less fuel in the tank, and water in the fuel can also cause problems. Thankfully there is not much humidity in the desert, but on the coast it can get bad at times. My reserve fuel tank on top of my tool box was almost full and, with a short length of hose, I let gravity feed over a hundred litres into my main running tank. This would be enough to get me the estimated 150 kilometres to Najran.

There did not seem to be much happening with the Army drivers; they were just sitting out the heat of the midday sun. For something to do I started climbing to the top of the rock outcrop. It was at least 30 metres to the top and I hoped for a good view and looked around for landmarks. The climbing was easy as the large boulders were smooth with many years of wind and sand storms having worn them down. Because of the heat haze, the horizon was rather obscure.

Looking to the south, there was nothing as far as the eye could see. To the west, where we were heading, I could just make out another rock outcrop. These did make very good landmarks. To the north there was the ever impenetrable Empty Quarter looking more daunting than ever. To the east, the way we had just come from, there was just the heat haze that obscured even the horizon, hiding the dusty town of Sharawrah.

At least up here, at the top of the rocks, there was a slight breeze, but it was so hot it seemed to burn you. Even the rocks were too hot to touch or sit on. I kept a good look out for snakes and scorpions, but did not see any. Maybe it was too hot for them, too, as they hunted mostly at night. I had been told the smaller scorpions had the deadliest sting, some with enough venom to kill you. The large scorpion's sting was apparently about the same strength as that of a bee. Well, bee stings hurt, so I never wanted to get that close to a scorpion to find out! I climbed carefully back down from the rocks, and got into my cab to make a cup of tea and eat a tin of peaches and cream crackers for lunch. When it was so hot I did not feel hungry, but thought I should eat something.

After eating there was still not much happening in the way of getting on the move again, and I was soon dozing off. I was dreaming of happily driving along a cool mountain ridge, when the engine blew up! What a hell of a way to wake up! I grabbed the steering wheel expecting a crash, and then realized it was not me at all, but the deafening sound of all six transporter engines starting up!

"Here we go again!" I thought.

I stayed a little way back out of the way of the dust they threw up, and to see where they were going. The only snag with this was if I broke down, no one was going to know and come back for me. It was best not to think about that happening.

The officer in charge certainly knew the best way, and how to pick a good route. We avoided any sand soft enough to get stuck in, and went on detours to go round higher sand dunes. We all stopped in the afternoon for 15 minutes for afternoon prayers then soon got going again. Towards dusk I thought we would maybe stop for the night, but the going was good and we all pressed on.

Just as it was getting dark, the last transporter I was following unexpectedly went through the narrow gap in the long sand dune. The journey was all done in one day! This made it look so easy! We were back in the village of Ukhdud, safe and sound. Compared to the journey out this had been a piece of cake, all 300 kilometres of desert in one day!

I left the Army transporters without even a "thank you" as they did not seem interested if I was still there or not. After I parked on the outskirts of town near the big room, it was less than a hundred metres walk back to the restaurant.

"Chicken and rice on the menu tonight," I thought. That would make a change from my dull food. Going back to my cab after a good meal, it was time to try and get some sleep.

Next morning I set off now knowing which way to go on the now familiar five kilometres to Najran. I parked next to my two loaded trailers, pleased with the success of the first load. I was also pleased to find that not a single thing had been touched on the two trailers. All the light fittings were still in place, and there were no signs of the loads being tampered with – if you stop for a meal or overnight in some other countries, even in England, the first things to go are the light fittings.

There was nobody about and, just in front of me, there was a trough of cool water. The Volvo truck engine was reliably pumping water 24 hours a day, as it supplied the large date plantation. Wearing only my shorts, I walked over the road with my soap and shampoo. What a luxury it was to wallow in the trough of cool water. I washed my hair and removed all the dirt and dust of the last few days. Getting out, I soon dried off in no time with just the heat of the day. The amount of water being pumped out would fill a bath in half a minute or less, so all the soap bubbles soon washed away. Any animals drinking after my dip would not get harmed. I did not see any camels or goats in Najran anyway, which was a bit unusual.

I now had one trailer delivered, and two to go. I hoped it would get easier with the knowledge I had gained so far, but it turned out to get even harder still.

So much to learn

I had a fitful night's sleep as it was so hot again. I was also thinking what my next move should be. My first job in the morning was to unhitch the empty trailer and hook up to the next loaded one. Then, using all the ropes and straps I had, I secured the following load down ready for the road, or, in this case, the desert.

I went to visit Ali in his house only 50 metres away. I tried to explain to him that I needed to buy some empty 200 litre drums. Describing chicken eggs would have been easier! Eventually, after pointing to his vehicle filler cap and miming the shape of a big drum, he understood me.

He drove me into Najran in his beaten up old Chevy pickup. I think the shock absorbers were totally worn out making it wallow at the slightest bump, but I expect that was why he liked it.

It was good to have at least one friend down here, even though we could hardly understand a word spoken between us except for the word beer! Ali took me to a vehicle service station in the middle of town. In Saudi Arabia, similar shops all seem to be in the same road or area, unlike in England. When you know what you want it makes it so much easier to find. There were quite a few people crossing the road with abandon, as there was very little traffic on the dusty road.

It was very rare to see any women about, and when you did it was not possible to see them properly as they were completely covered, wearing their all-black burka and hijab. Often the women also had what seemed like a leather beak covering their nose. Even their eyes were obscured by black netting.

Having drums of spare fuel was something I should have taken on the first trip, but you learn as you go along. Thinking about it, on the last trip, if I had been unaware of a leak in the main fuel tank, it would have caused a big problem. But then as long as I had diesel fuel in the spare tank, I could have rigged up a pipe from that to the fuel pump. There is often a way round such problems.

Once, when I was working for the firm Astran, I had a leak in my fuel tank on the mountainous dirt roads of Eastern Turkey. I was miles away from any town and unable to get a repair. There was nothing else I could do but drive on until I reached the next town. Fortunately in Turkey every town had a garage and a useful blacksmith. Before all the fuel ran out from a six inch split on the bottom of the tank, I rubbed soap into the crack until the leak stopped. This temporary repair got me to a blacksmith in the next town. There the fuel tank was taken off the chassis and a tin patch was braised over the crack. It looked a very dangerous job as the blacksmith did the work, and luckily it did not blow up. An excellent repair was made which lasted for a long time.

The service garage at Najran was next door to a gas bottle refuelling shop. That was worth remembering, as I use camping gas to fuel my cooker. Once, when getting my gas bottle refuelled in Jeddah, the man doing it connected a long pipe from a big tank onto my bottle. After a while, he opened a valve above my gas bottle to let some of the gas pressure out, and then I assumed was able to put more liquid gas in. He was smoking a cigarette as he squatted in front of my bottle, and let some gas escape several times. I stood well back, expecting him to disappear in a big whoosh of flames, but thankfully nothing happened.

Meanwhile, at the service garage there was a yard at the back where there were stacks of empty 200 litre oil drums. I chose three of the best, that were hardly dented and had screw filler caps. With Ali's help, and a bit of bargaining, I finally paid the exorbitant amount of 25 riyals each – a total cost of about £75. The drums cost a lot more than I expected but luckily to fill them up would only cost about £8. We loaded the empty drums onto Ali's pickup truck.

My next stop was the bank as my cash supply of local money was nearly exhausted. I had American dollar traveller's cheques which I changed into Saudi riyals. I always got a good rate of exchange with dollars, and never had any trouble. Dollars were much preferred to pounds sterling.

Next, I went to a food store where I bought lots of water, plus some tins of fish, meat, fruit and biscuits. Finally, back at my truck and three trailers, we unloaded the drums and I thanked Ali. I then had to work out how to fill the drums and secure them onto the next loaded trailer.

The empty drums were easy to pull up to the top of the load with a rope, and I was able to find a good place for them amongst all the crates. I roped them on securely, as they could end up as my lifeline. On the outskirts of Najran I knew of a filling station, and I was able to get close enough to fill the two green drums with diesel.

Luckily the garage had a water hose and this I used to fill the blue drum. The garage owner wanted more money for the water than the fuel! By letting the water overflow I got some of the oil out. A little oily tasting water was no hardship if that was all there was to drink. It was only for emergencies, so hopefully would never be needed. It would also make a good standby for the large radiator on the truck.

All three drums were not quite full, allowing for expansion, and the filler cap was not done up too tightly. I knew I would have to keep an eye on them as I did not want them to split. I must say I felt much happier with these reserves. I now had enough fuel to pay back the Air Force at Sharawrah, and enough for me to get there and back with some to spare. I never gave it a thought on the first trip, how stupid!

The next problem would be much harder to solve, and a little out of my hands. How was I going to get help in getting to Sharawrah with the second trailer? Next day Ali took me to Ukhdud in his Toyota Crown 4 x 4. His old pickup only had rear wheel drive, and would be useless across the soft sand.

Then we were back again in the big room with about 20 smartly-dressed men in their Arab attire. This time there would be no chai to drink as Ramadan had started. During the month of Ramadan for all Muslims there is no eating, drinking or smoking allowed in the hours of daylight. As I was a non-Muslim it did not affect me, but I never ate or drank in the daytime if there was any possible chance of being seen.

For two hours in the big room there was lots of talk. As to whether my problem was discussed or not I had no idea. I kept quiet as did a few of the others. The head man at the end of the room did most of the talking. I never did find out if going to the big room helped, or maybe they just wanted to see me! Ali took me back to my truck – another day was gone with little to show for it.

Next day, after another very hot night, it was a case of just waiting around. In the afternoon Ali took me to Najran, and showed me into the prince's palace. Luckily I had a T-shirt and long trousers on, which I always wore so as not to offend anyone. I still felt much underdressed compared to everyone else in their long gleaming white robes and head dress.

I was shown into a windowless room about 10' square with a bed, chair and a prayer mat. One bare light bulb lit the room: it was all a bit gloomy. A small dusty skylight did little to brighten things up. A picture of the ruler of Saudi Arabia on the wall was the only decoration. The mattress on the bed was just about comfortable with a blanket if needed. There was no air conditioning, so it was very hot and stuffy.

The whole palace was built on one floor, and had no elaborate mosaics or finery. I had no toilet things or any personal things with me, as I had not known that this was to be my home for the next couple of nights. At least there was a towel in my room, and soap in the communal washroom along the hall. The toilets in another room were just holes in the floor, with no paper. Instead there was a short length of hose with a tap for cleaning yourself. I found my way about by wandering along the bare dusty hallways. It was not at all grand for a prince's palace.

Not long after it got dark I was ushered with some other guests into a long room with a big wooden table in the middle. The table was big enough for 20 people, but there were only 12 of us there at that moment. We each had a plate with a spoon and fork, but there were no knives. In the middle of the table there were bowls of rice and half a dozen cooked whole chickens. There were jugs of water available to pour into our plain glasses.

I spooned some rice onto my plate, and knew that you only use your right hand to pull at the chicken. I ate my rice with my spoon but most of my companions squeezed their rice into a ball. This was a bit messy but they were better at it than I would have been. There was not much conversation. Nobody attempted to talk to me, and I felt a bit out of it. The penny dropped at midnight when we were all ushered back into the dining room with a similar meal in front of us. At five in the morning before dawn we were back again for breakfast. This consisted of flat bread with jam or honey and lots of chai. I always enjoyed the flat bread. It was crispy and had a nice flavour. It was a pity it did not keep fresh for long, only half a day if you were lucky.

So that was how to fast during Ramadan, reverse day with night. It looked as if I would have to try and sleep for the rest of the day. Nothing happened at all that day, making it a long, boring time. I wished I had a book to read. I dared not go out anywhere in case that was when I was wanted.

Eventually it got dark. I was more thirsty than hungry when I went into the dining room. The same men were there and again I was completely ignored. For a change it was chicken and rice! I was glad I liked chicken, and the rice was very tasty.

After the meal, not long after going back to my room, I was invited into the prince's interview room. What a contrast after all the drabness! There were beautiful rugs on the floor and on all the walls. The prince sat on an ornate chair on a raised platform. Everyone else had colourful cushions to squat cross-legged on. With nearly 20 men in the room it was getting very full.

After waiting 10 minutes, a man who spoke German arrived as my interpreter. It was just as well I could speak enough German to be understood. What with a French man last time, I wondered if they knew what nationality I was! I explained that I needed to go to Sharawrah. This seemed to confuse everyone as at first they thought I had not yet been. I explained that I had been once but needed to go twice more. I told him there were two trailers still to go. He told the prince what I wanted. Finally the message was understood. At last some progress made. I also explained that I needed a letter to get me to Sharawrah and back again to Najran, but the last bit did not seem to get through.

Two different Bedouins came into the room. With their old Lee Enfield rifles and bandoliers of bullets criss-crossed over their chests they looked like quite formidable bodyguards. These Bedouins were to be my guides on the next trip I was told. When I asked when we would be leaving, I was told bukra.

"Tomorrow, give or take a day or two!" I thought.

I stayed for the midnight meal and breakfast before leaving next morning. Just before leaving I was given a letter all in Arabic which I understood to be my authorisation to go to Sharawrah. Whether it would get me back again was another thing!

Thankfully I got a lift to go the four kilometres back to my truck. Once there, I pulled the curtains round in my cab and had a refreshing coffee. Ali's home was not far away, so I went over to say "Salaam alaykum". There would be no trips into town for a beer during Ramadan.

Usually he came out to greet me, but this time I was invited in. There were three women in colourful robes, who I guessed were his wives. They were sitting in a semicircle in front of Ali. There were lots of colourful rugs on the floor, quite a contrast to the sand outside. I nodded and said "Salaam alaykum" to his wives and squatted down near to Ali.

Ali was not very happy, and despite our language problem it turned out he had toothache. I had lots of Paracetamol tablets in my cab and went back to my truck to get a packet. I know the Arabic numbers one to ten and explained to the youngest wife (she was more attractive that the other two!) that Ali should take two tablets, four times a day. Because it was Ramadan he could not see a dentist.

In the afternoon I drove with the second loaded trailer across to Ukhdud. It was so easy finding my way now that I knew which way to go. There was no re-freshing water trough, but a restaurant to eat in after it was dark. Everything was out of my hands now, I just had to be patient and wait. This was all taking a lot longer than I had thought.

I waited for two long, hot days swatting flies, never wanting to go far from my truck in case something happened. On the morning of the third day, the two Bedouins I had met at the prince's palace drove up in a 4 x 4. I started the engine to build up the air pressure all ready to go, but with no sign of moving switched off and waited again.

Then an hour later, to my surprise, an American 6 x 6 Army truck pulled up just ahead of me. There were three soldiers in the cab and three in the back. Also in the back of the Army truck there were four goats and two bags of rice. That's what you call meals on wheels! After some talking between the Bedouins and the soldiers, everyone got into their respective vehicles and started to move off. At last we were on the move again, and this time I had some idea of what lay ahead.

Army escort... what next?

We all drove out through the gap in the sand dune. First the 4 x 4, then the Army truck, followed by me. This time I drove without so much trepidation on the now more familiar desert.

I looked in my mirror, mainly to see if my load was secure, when I saw that we were being followed by another vehicle. I did not expect that! And I wondered what it could be. It was difficult to see with all the dust trailing behind me. By letting the vehicle catch up, it started to pull alongside, and I could see that it was a big six-wheeled fuel tanker.

"The more the merrier," I thought.

As usual it was easy going for a couple of hours, and it was good to be moving again. Apart from one stop for prayers and nearly getting stuck in soft sand we made good progress. At one place, as we weaved our way around some 20' high sand dunes, I could distinctly make out my tyre marks from the previous trip. As I followed them on the hard sand between two sand dunes I could see my old tyre tracks turned to the left, and completely disappeared under a big sand dune. That sand dune was obviously not there a couple of weeks ago. Thousands, if not millions, of tons of sand had shifted in just that short time!

By midday we had travelled about 80 kilometres. The Army truck did not go as fast as I would like, but then I realised we would probably be travelling into Yemen some of the way. We were not always in Saudi Arabia as I at first thought. This was one of the reasons the Army truck and soldiers were with us I supposed. In that respect it was reassuring to have their company.

After three hours and another stop for prayers we arrived at the first outcrop of rocks. We all sat in the shade of a huge rock a couple of metres out from the main rocks. For over two hours some of the soldiers slept while I swatted flies, and wished it was not so hot!

Two of the Bedouins got up and went racing off around a large rock. I did not see what they did, but they came back with a long thin snake. It was dead now and I did not know if it normally had a flat head or the Bedouins had reshaped it.

Bedouins holding a dead snake

As everyone was starting to show some movement, I asked one of the Bedouins how to write my name in Arabic. Then with a marker pen I wrote my name on the large rock. Although I wrote it high up I expect the first sand storm obliterated it. They had prayers again before everyone started to get ready to move off. I was sitting in the cab ready to go this time. The next thing I knew was that one of the Bedouins had a goat on the ground at the side of my cab. He slit its throat, using one of two sharp knives they all wear on their belts. Within a couple of minutes the goat was dead with no crying out, which I was glad about!

It did not take long to bleed the animal and have it skinned. With its back legs tied together with sinew, it was then hung on the front corner of my trailer where I could see it in my mirror! All a bit blood thirsty for me, but when living in the wild it's live or die! When we stopped later at the next rock outcrop I was surprised there were no flies on the carcass.

At every opportunity bits of wood were collected apart from some brought with us from the beginning. Soon a fire was made and with the meat cut up and put in one bowl, and rice in another bowl a meal was made ready in a couple of hours.

While the meal was cooking I climbed to the top of the rock outcrop, this time being more aware of snakes, scorpions and owls. As it was a little cooler there was less heat haze and it was possible to see much further. Nothing moved in any direction. All I could see was a lot of desert. I climbed carefully down as the rocks were still very hot to the touch.

When the meal was ready to be served, we all squatted down in a circle near the fire. No plates or spoons this time. Then the food was dished up on two big metal plates, and we all helped ourselves. The rice was squeezed into a ball with your right hand and popped into your mouth. The legs of the goat still had their joints and, with right hand only, the Muslim way, I could see it was sometimes quite an effort to get the joint to break. I enjoy eating off the bone, and although my hand got all messy it turned out to be a very

Looking down onto the tanker and Army truck

enjoyable meal. I managed to get one joint separated with a tug, pull and twist with a Bedouin, which pleased me. It felt good to be together eating like this.

A few months before, when driving on the road to Buraydah in Saudi Arabia, I had stopped at a roadside mud shack for a meal. It was a good sign for a place to stop as a couple of trucks were already parked nearby. There were no utensils served with the meal, so I ate a whole small chicken and rice with my hands. It gives a whole new concept to eating food. Not just taste and smell, but feel too.

When the meal with the soldiers and two Bedouins was over and everything tidied up, we all sat round the fire just before dusk. Nobody had a light or a torch, so everything had to be done in daylight or by the light of the fire after dark. One of the soldiers was interested in the gold St. Christopher on a chain round my neck. It depicted St. Christopher carrying Jesus across a stream. The Qu'ran mentions Jesus so they knew what it meant in a way. I tried to explain it meant a safe journey for travellers, but that was too difficult to explain so I left it as a representation of Jesus. I think they were pleased I had some religion. This trip was so much more friendly and enjoyable than last time. At last I could relax and feel safe.

Suddenly one of the Bedouins got up and started hitting the sand with his flip flop! For a moment I thought he had gone mad, until I too got up and saw this big spider he had killed with his sandal. I found out later that it was a camel spider, and can grow to the size of a hand. This was not a very pleasant creature. Normally they attack camels at night by numbing the skin and then eating it.

Photo of a camel spider

I once saw an Arab with most of his bottom lip missing, exposing the gum and teeth. This was the result of a camel spider bite while he slept. Arabs often sleep on the desert floor if they are miles from anywhere. Seeing the size of this spider I was glad I always slept in the cab or on top of the trailer. Creepy crawlies were one of the bad elements about sleeping in the desert. On the plus side it is always very peaceful and quiet. Apart from the mosquitoes that is!

We were now one day out on this trip and still barely halfway there. To do it in one day now seemed like a dream. Next morning, after prayers, we got on the move again, going into the sun, which to me was roughly east. The going was good, with not enough soft stretches to get any of us stuck. I still had my tyre pressures at about 60 pounds per square inch but I don't think the Army truck had done anything to their tyres as, unlike me, they had no means of pumping them up again.

At one point I came to the top of a very long drop down to a flat valley below. This time I did not get caught out and took a good look to see what alternatives there were. The ridge went a long way in each direction and did not look as steep as the previous scary drop. The drop over was not too sheer and I decided that with care I could safely get to the bottom. It was easier than I thought and halfway down I stopped and took a photo.

The Army truck stayed at the top and the soldiers watched me get safely down but did not follow. Instead they went along the top and an hour later came into view having found a safer way down. We diverted round some big sand dunes by going even further south, and were able to keep up a fairly good average speed. If you did not check the milometer every now and again you would not think any distance had been travelled.

"This is going well," I thought.

As I drove a little behind and to one side of the Army truck, I noticed a change in the colour of the sand ahead to a lighter shade. The Army truck soon threw up more sand and dust and started to get bogged in. I eased off the throttle and engaged all three diff-locks.

Stopped half way down the long slope

Checking the depth of the tyre track in the sand before stopping

You are supposed to stop to engage the diff-locks, but I found that as long as all the wheels were going at the same speed, no harm was done. I was keeping straight and after the three green lights next to the diff-lock button came on, I put my foot down. The extra speed and grip got me across the 200 metres of really soft sand, and onto some firmer ground.

The Army truck was not so lucky and got stuck three quarters of the way across. I drove round in a big circle, as any sharp turns would put more drag on the two trailer axles. Fixing a long tow rope I soon had him pulled out and going again.

I would never have thought sand could have so many different textures. Sometimes it is so hard there is hardly any trace left behind, and any speed is possible. Then within a short distance it is so soft you sink in up to the axles. Once, on another desert crossing, I had to cross a short stretch that was like cement dust. Stepping in it my foot disappeared up to my calf with no resistance at all, it was so fine. It was almost like quicksand.

The fuel tanker got stuck as well as he only had drive to his rear two axles, unlike my truck with all three axles. I was surprised he had got this far without getting stuck before, he must have been an experienced driver.

We dug some of the sand away from the front of his tyres and, with the use of a long chain he had, I managed to tow him out of the soft sand.

What with the others getting stuck and the slow progress on the soft sand, it was late afternoon before the undulating gravel and stones came into view. The last few kilometres to Sharawrah, although noisy and bumpy, at least had no more surprises.

The fuel tanker drove up to the airport main gate, and eventually drove inside. It was too late for me to get unloaded, so I parked near the gates so as to be seen. Now was a good time for me to make a drink and eat a meal without worrying if I suddenly had to get moving again.

So as to stretch my legs I had a walk around Sharawrah, but it was as quiet and deserted as ever. Even the bank was closed and, towards dusk, I went back to my cab. I had some easy listening tapes and Abba's latest to keep me company. By 8 o'clock it was getting dark but still very hot at 50°C, that is 120°F, or as I call it, "blooming hot!"

I find any temperature above body heat seems to upset the system a bit. The body is so used to keeping warm that it does not know how to cool down except by sweating. On the occasions when I exert myself, that's when the sweat runs down into my eyes, it then stings and blurs my vision. It was so hot and dry out there that the body does not seem to sweat that much, but must be losing fluid at an alarming rate as it evaporates. Maybe I was not drinking enough, as I often craved for salt. To supplement this deficiency I cut up tomatoes, and ate them with a sprinkling of salt. Soon afterwards I always felt better, so it must have worked. I had no tomatoes this time, and it was too hot to eat much anyway.

With the second trailer here, the job was halfway done, but it was all taking such a long time. I was losing track of the days, it must have been nearly a month since I had left Jeddah. I had no idea of the date, or what day of the week it was. There was no chance of speeding things up, so I would just have to take one day at a time.

By now I knew that my load was all the equipment needed to build and install an Instrument Landing System for planes, known as ILS. Foreigners in Saudi Arabia like me were not allowed anything to do with military equipment. It was a bit late now to worry about that, but I wondered how on earth White Trux had got a job that was so sensitive. Maybe no other transport company wanted the job, or could not do the job. I could see now why it was a job best avoided with 300 kilometres of tricky desert to cross.

Thinking about it, I realised I was driving illegally, sometimes through Yemen, with over £2,000,000 worth of military equipment which I wasn't allowed to carry.

"Best not to think about it, and just do the best I can," I thought.

Thinking back to the office in Jeddah just before I left, I remembered some words of advice which were spoken to me: "Keep a low profile as best you can."

It did not mean much to me at the time. How do you keep a low profile with three big loaded trucks? Now I also knew what was also meant by: "And don't tell anyone what you have loaded." The situation for me did not look good, especially if I was stopped by the authorities.

"What have I got into now?" I thought. Then again I did wonder how many strings were being pulled behind my back, even by the prince in Najran. Now I could see why the soldiers were with me!

It was time to try and get some sleep, and not to worry about anything. Ha, ha!

Two down, one to go

I had another very hot night trying to get some sleep. It seemed even hotter here than in Najran, so I was pleased when finally a new day dawned. Getting through the gate was the first hurdle. I showed my load details and letter to travel to the guard – in return I got some funny looks. The guard would not let me in, and the gates stayed closed. It was possible he could not read or maybe understand the documents as he went into the guard house and showed the paperwork to his colleague. This guard read the two bits of paper, then used the phone. Meanwhile I was blocking the entrance. I made my mind up that no one was going to get in or out until my problem was resolved. I had a lot of faith in my British passport – if it was good enough to stop any bullets I was not sure.

The officer that helped me the first time came after an hour. In no time the gate was opened and I drove in and parked near the previous delivery of crates. Before the officer walked off I told him I had the 200 litres of fuel for him, which pleased him. I took off all the straps and ropes and waited in the hot sun.

After a couple of hours (at least it was the same day), the machine with the large three metre wide bucket arrived. As before, I pushed and levered the large crates into or at least onto the bucket. All the cases were marked fragile, with a picture of a glass to emphasize this. Not only that, but on each side of each case there were stencilled "This way up" arrows. Needless to say, just like last time, the crates were often dropped from a height of a meter or so, and landed on their sides. The smaller ones even landed upside down. No attempt was made to right anything and I was even past caring about it myself now. The hardest item to unload was a two metre square metal fuel tank. I had to strap that onto the bucket to hold it on. After over three hours in the sweltering heat everything was unloaded and I just needed to have my three drums put back on the trailer. With no head board on the front of the trailer, they were going to need a lot of securing.

I drove next to what look like a workshop to give back the 200 litres of fuel. I did not want to give away my expensive oil barrel so asked for a pump to transfer the fuel. After lots of sign language, a hand pump was produced. I checked that the pipe from the pump in the drum was going into a tank of diesel; you can smell it a mile off! Then I started pumping. By then I felt I had done enough for one day and parked next to the crates.

I take a pride in a job well done, and I thought just getting here twice was good going. To have the load just dumped on the sand to make some goats more comfortable was beyond me.

I put the kettle on to make a well-earned cup of tea and sat in the cab to see if I could get the World Service on the radio. Just hearing Big Ben was music to my ears. I was just starting to relax, when a "bang bang" on my driver's door made me jump, I nearly spilt my tea!

A young man in western dress was standing next to my truck. I jumped out to shake his hand and say hello.

"Howdy" he said in an American accent, so I guessed he was American with no trouble. I offered him a cup of tea or coffee, but he declined.

On asking what he was doing in this far-out place, the answer did not surprise me. In Saudi Arabia anything was possible! He told me he had installed a weather station in the far corner of the air field, and that the battery to power the equipment was charged by a mini nuclear reactor.

"Wow, I bet that was not cheap," I thought.

There was only one snag, he told me. The 12 metre high mast for the aerial that sent a signal to the tower needed a red light on top. Any structure over a certain height needed a red light on top at air fields. The nuclear generator could not supply the extra power required for the light and the battery kept getting drained. To solve the problem, an electric cable was going to be laid for two kilometres from the power house to supply the extra power needed. In that case, I thought, no need to have the nuclear power supply, but mine was not to reason why!

It was good to talk to someone in English. There had not been much work done during Ramadan so that for him the three day job was taking three weeks or more already. He could not wait to get home, and was hoping to leave in a couple of days. I asked him how he was planning to get back to America. When he said via London Heathrow, I thought to myself that that was good, maybe he could post a letter home for me. I wrote the letter, addressed to my home in Maidstone, Kent and offered him money for the stamp, but he declined any payment. Whether it arrived or not I never found out, so it was quite possible the letter did not get posted. It was now over a month since I had left Jeddah at the start of this job, and since then I had had no way of telling the office or my wife at home that I was alright. Everything was taking a long time, but I was hopeful that it would have a happy ending.

Another hot day slid by and nothing happened. Maybe it was Friday, like our Sunday. I had lost track of the days of the week. Come to think of it, the days of the month, too.

Through experience of being stuck at border crossings in the Middle East, I know that it pays to be a bit of a nuisance, and so it seemed I was with me being parked inside the perimeter fence. An officer came the next afternoon asking me to park outside. I expect they thought I was a security risk. I asked the officer if I could please talk to the camp commanding officer.

Together we went to the control tower and, after waiting an hour, I was shown into an adjoining room. With the help of the English speaking officer I explained there was still one more trailer in Najran to be delivered to this airport. For safety I needed an escort back, possibly with the Bedouins and soldiers I had come out with. To me it did not seem too much to ask. The two officers had a discussion, the outcome of which was bukra, and would I park outside the perimeter today!

The roads in Sharawrah were too narrow to drive down so I parked on the edge of town nearer to Najran. If any vehicles did leave I would hopefully see them. Late afternoon, and not expecting anything to set off at this time of day, I walked into town heading for the bank, but it was all closed. It seemed odd that there were no chai shops or any shops selling things. It was almost like a ghost town and as it got dark all the more spooky. It was a relief to get back in my cab with the radio for company. Good old BBC World Service!

The middle of the next morning, one of the Bedouins drove up in his Toyota and spoke lots of Arabic to me, of which I understood only one word, bukra. Then he drove off back into Sharawrah. I never saw any vehicles in Sharawrah, the dirt roads were too narrow to park in, so I guessed they parked inside one of the metal gates in front of each property.

While waiting for bukra I filled my main fuel tank from one of the barrels on the front of the trailer. I was now all ready to go. The rest of the fuel in the barrels was for emergencies, and I hoped not to have to use them too much as I thought they might be somewhat contaminated. I also felt happier to have the barrel of water with me even though it was not pure. I was down to my last three bottles of drinking water, and needed to replenish them very soon.

The next morning I woke up really early as the sun was rising. It's a very pleasant time in the coolest part of the day before the flies wake up. I could see why Arabs are known to go walking about for 24 hours to clear the mind and relax. As I sat with the door open looking at the flat open desert, there was nothing moving, nothing to see. That's enough to make the mind go blank. It is supposed to be good for you like meditating.

I snapped out of my dream and quickly back to reality. My first thoughts were, will I be going today, and what else can I do to speed things up? I had just resigned myself to another wasted day when two vehicles came out of Sharawrah.

It turned out to be the best bukra ever when the two Bedouins and six young soldiers in the Army truck came slowly past. With oil and water levels checked, the barrels secure on the trailer, I even had the air built up. I was soon on their trail. It was good to be driving again. I have always enjoyed driving, no matter where I go and in whatever type of vehicle, but the desert has more excitement to it than anywhere, not knowing what will happen next.

I tagged along behind, having no trouble keeping up now I was not loaded. Our three vehicles, spread out at times, made good progress and after three hours we had done nearly a hundred kilometres, a third of the way already.

We must have gone a different way back, and I guess even more into Yemen. At least the going was firm and at one point we passed a burnt out Army vehicle left over from the last war. No scrap merchants out here!

Parked by a burnt out wreck

About midday we stopped for prayers, and, still on good firm sand, got going again. It seemed to be getting even hotter and a breeze sprang up. Then, in the distance, a huge tall cloud came towards us from the south. Soon the wind was howling and in no time we were all enveloped in a sandstorm. Even with the windows closed the fine dust got into the cab. It was impossible to see to drive and we all stopped before the worst arrived. I switched the engine off to stop the air filter getting clogged up, and parked side on to the wind.

Once when driving in Iraq I was caught in a sand storm. After it had blown out the front bumper had all the paint taken off and the headlight glass had gone completely opaque. This time I took the glass out and cut thick plastic covers to make the head-lights usable.

The fine dust got even worse in the cab so I dampened a towel to wrap round my face. The fine dust and grit got everywhere, even in my mouth and ears. How long sandstorms last I was soon to find out. This one blew itself out in a couple of hours. Soon the dust settled, the sun shone again and it was as if nothing had happened.

The desert can be so quiet. Without the engine running, it was as if I had lost my hearing. It made a change to hear the wind, but a pity about the sand and dust to spoil things. The air felt a little cooler for a while, but that did not last long. Apart from that weather event, every day was a clear blue sky without a cloud in sight. I missed the clouds.

We got on our way again but soon came up against a 500' high ridge of soft sand. It seemed to stretch for miles in either direction so I thought it worth having a go to get to the top. Now I had no load I had plenty of power to spare and the chances of getting to the top looked very hopeful. Anyway I like a challenge!

Going up close to the base of the ridge I had a good look at the possibilities. The first half was a gentle slope

View of the Empty Quarter dunes

of maybe 20° with no big dips. Nearer the top it was steeper and the dips got more severe which could be a problem. As long as I did not go parallel and risk turning over, it seemed worth giving it a try.

Distances are deceptive in the desert, so I checked when I had gone three kilometres away from the base and made a U-turn to face this next hurdle in my travels. Even from this distance it looked quite formidable. When I was driving on good hard sand, I had all three of the diff-locks disengaged. This time I needed all the help I could get. The tyres were already at a lower pressure. I made sure all three diff-locks were engaged. A small green light by each button stayed on. After taking a drink of warm water I was ready to go.

Up through the gears to eighth and doing nearly 90kph I was still a kilometre away. There was one place ahead where the sand made a gentler slope to start with and I aimed for that. I knew that once the wheels started to spin I would have to give up. Easing off the power on such a steep slope would soon bring me to a stop. Without the trailer dragging me back I was sure I could fly up to the top with no trouble. As it was, a third of the way up I had to change down a gear, and soon down another gear. Down to 60kph, but slowing fast. The hopes of getting to the top started to fade.

Getting only halfway up would be worse than not going up at all. With the steepness of the sand it would be dangerous to attempt a U-turn. The tyres on the lower side would dig in more, making the truck lean over dangerously. That would risk rolling over and over all the way to the bottom. Reversing carefully was the only choice.

There was still not much wheel spin but I was going slower, and still only halfway up. I was now getting to where there was a big dip on either side. The one to the right looked bigger, being a hundred metres across.

By turning into it I was now going down and able to pick up speed again. Using the big curve of the dip like a wall of death and now with more momentum I sped nearly to the top of the dip on the other side. As I slowed, I was able to turn around to face downhill and able to pick up speed again.

The momentum of the truck stopped it wanting to roll over as I turned and where the dip was not so steep I charged up the ridge. Each time with this manoeuvre I was getting nearer to the top. It was great fun, like driving a sand buggy except I was in a big truck. Instead of the dips being a hindrance they proved to be just what was needed to get me nearer to the top. With only ten metres left to go, I dived down one more dip and got over the top feeling well pleased with myself!

There was a great view from the top to the east, but there was no sign of the Bedouins or the Army truck. This was a good time to put the kettle on and have a well-earned cup of afternoon tea!

After over an hour, both vehicles came into view having found an easier way round. The sun was on the way down when we stopped for the night at one of the rock outcrops. They must be a remnant of a volcanic period many thousands of years ago. It seemed strange that on the first trip we did not go anywhere near any big drops. Then I remembered nearly driving over one and having to reverse away from it. Maybe that was the same one. I had learnt a lot about the desert since then!

On one long stretch of hard sand we came across a burnt out six-wheeled army personnel carrier. It was all rusty and had no tyres left. There must have been armies fighting here once, probably in the last war.

Being late in the day it looked as if we were going to stop the night here. This time there was no goat and rice. The goats must have either been sold or eaten in Sharawrah. I had a tin of tuna with cream crackers followed by peaches in syrup and a cup of coffee. I tried to sleep, knowing that the last stretch to Najran should not be too difficult. I started to doze wondering if Ali was alright taking the pills for his toothache.

Next day, there was another clear blue sky and we got underway again after prayers. I saw another mirage. They are very weird. It is like driving towards a blue lake in the distance, but never getting any nearer. We stopped for prayers at the second rock outcrop, and, being near midday, had a two-hour stop over.

I wished I could have had a siesta, but I was still wary of being left behind. We were soon on the move again and, after a while, we were close to the high sand dunes to the north, and then before I knew it we came to the sandy gap into Ukhdud. It was well hidden, and could only be seen when right on top of it.

The Army truck kept going, on its way back to Najran I guess. With Ramadan over, the restaurant was open, and I treated myself to a whole small chicken (I don't think they did halves anyway) with rice and a Pepsi. Feeling full I drove back to my last loaded trailer. Nothing had been touched. A week of leaving it in England would have had the light fittings and a wheel or two gone walkabout!

First things first! I intended to have a dip in the cool water trough to get all the dust out of my hair and off my body. I did not have many spare clothes, so they got washed too. It was as I was drying off that I remembered giving Ali the codeine tablets. Supposing he had had a bad reaction to the pills! My life would not be worth living. The only way to find out was to go to his home and see.

Feeling rather nervous I knocked on the door. Joy of joys! Ali opened the wooden door and, with a big smile, invited me into his home. His three wives were in the same chairs and this time I shook hands instead of exchanging just a nod. It was fairly dull in the room, with only one window to let the light in. All three wives were dressed in colourful long robes and had lots of bracelets and beads. They all looked very happy that I had helped Ali's toothache. It would not have been much fun living with a man with toothache for two weeks!

Ali ushered me out into his old pickup and we were off to Najran to the non-alcoholic beer shop. Ali showed me a gap in his teeth – the dentist had sorted him out while I was away.

The shop also sold bottled water, so I took the opportunity to restock. I had saved my empty bottles and intended to fill them up at the trough where the water was drawn up from the ground. It looked very clean but to be on the safe side I put in some purification tablets.

Back at my truck I unhitched the empty trailer, and got the last trailer raised enough to get my truck under. After fixing all the straps and ropes on this last load, it was all ready to go. That evening I tried to work out how to go about setting off on the last trip.

Learning the meaning of "bukra"

After a restless night chasing mosquitoes, I managed to get a few hours' sleep towards dawn. If going to the palace had got things moving last time, it seemed a good idea to go there again. I waited until Ali came out of his house and indicated to him my wish to go into Najran. With Ramadan over this would be a chance for Ali to indulge in a non-alcoholic beer or two. I was starting to think of it as "the booze cruise". Not quite the same as going across the channel for crates of beer and wine, but the next best thing down here. I thanked Ali for the lift into town, and started walking towards the palace.

In the centre of town everybody was walking towards the mosque for midday prayers. I was the only one going the other way, and soon found the doorway to the prince's palace at the end of a narrow alleyway. It was certainly not very elaborate, and could be the door to anybody's home. There was nobody to stop me at the door, so I walked straight in and along the corridor to see if the room I had last time was empty. It was empty, so I made myself at home, and thought how I would go about getting some attention.

My thinking was that if I pretended I was invited, and kept asking to see the "chief" eventually I would get to see the prince. Then hopefully they would find someone who could interpret my wishes for another, final, trip to Sharawrah. To get things done in this part of the world it sometimes pays to barge in, I have often observed.

By evening I heard lots of moving around and hoped it was meal time. Going into the large dining room with the long bare wooden table, I got some funny looks! By making it look as if I was invited and doing my best to look confident, I sat down at the table amongst the robed guests. There was not a lot of talking, as they did not seem to know each other, which suited me. After the meal of chicken and rice, everybody got up and left, so I went back to my room hoping some comment would get me to higher places.

Breakfast of flat bread and jam went by, so did lunch with rice and chicken for a change. I had just fallen asleep in my room when there was a knock on the door and I was ushered into the prince's lush room. There were about a dozen Saudis in the room. The prince was sitting on his raised chair in the middle of the back wall. I said, "Salaam alaykum," and shook hands with everyone. The room was very colourful after the drabness of the rest of the building. There was a lot of talking, all in Arabic, of which I never understood a word. Nobody looked pleased to see me; it was as if I was a nuisance, and they were wondering how to get rid of me.

I knew the word in Arabic for truck was something like "searra". It meant a thing with wheels which was good enough for me. During a short lull in the conversation I got the prince's attention. By pretending to drive and saying, "Searra Sharawrah!" I hoped to get my message across. I was going to have to tough this out if I was to get the job finished. No interpreter came and with a wave of the hand it was indicated I should leave.

Back at my room I had all sorts of thoughts on how I could have done it better. Not speaking the language was a big problem down here where only a few, if any, foreigners came. In the marketplace in Jeddah all the traders spoke English. The few words of Arabic I knew plus the numbers were useful at the little shacks at the side of the road when buying food and goods, but not a lot of good here.

I lay on my bed and a couple of fretful hours slowly passed by. Then there was another knock on the door. Feeling some trepidation, I was ushered out of my room. If we turned left at the end of the corridor we would go to the prince's room, if we turned right I would be out of the front door, on my ear, so to speak. We turned left, this was a good start!

The man who spoke German was there again. It seems they did not understand why I needed to go to Sharawrah yet again. I explained about the three trailers, and that this was the last one to go. Luckily I was not asked what my load was – that could have caused even more trouble. On the other hand, they may have known anyway.

When two Bedouins came into the room my hopes soared. The two were not as burly as the others, but as long as they knew the way I did not care. Now at last we were getting somewhere. This second visit seemed to go much better and there were a few smiles as I said, "Shukran" (meaning "thank you"). I asked when would we be leaving as I was about to leave the room. In reply, I was told bukra. I'd heard that before!

The thought of staying overnight at the palace did not impress me, so I left the palace and started walking back out of town. It took me just over an hour in the heat of the day before I got back to my truck. I felt pleased with how things had gone at the palace – the last trip to Sharawrah was more of a reality now.

I had the ignition key in my pocket, but my truck door was never locked. With my fingers crossed that the powers that be had got the message, I would just have to wait and hope for the best. I decided to stay here for the night. I had plenty of food, and the water trough across the road was a good incentive to stay.

It was good to be sleeping in my own bed, albeit in the truck. No coughing and other noises to disturb me for one thing. Next day I was in two minds about staying at the end of the tarmac road, but the previous two journeys had started at Ukhdud, so decided to drive there later in the day. There was nobody about to object, so first I took a dip in the water trough. With my hair washed and teeth cleaned I was ready for another day. I dried off in the heat of the sun in no time – there was no need to use a towel.

The drive to Ukhdud was easier to find than ever, except that with so many vehicles going back and forth it was impossible not to go in other vehicles' tracks. The tall clumps of grassy sand were everywhere and I had to weave in and out of them most of the way. I parked on the edge of the village as before, with a tall embankment of rocks on one side and another of rocks and sand in front. The embankment made a good barrier to stop the moving sand swamping the village.

I waited all day, but nothing happened. Nobody came even to say bukra so to keep my spirits up I said, "Bukra inshala" ("tomorrow God willing") to myself. The next day was the same as the day before. I was very tempted to go back to where the trailers were parked, just to have a dip in the trough and cool down for a few minutes. But I knew the local people were aware of me being here so I decided to stay put and keep hoping for the best. There were no telephone lines out of Ukhdud, and this was well before mobile phones were invented.

I was really getting bored and the time dragged by so slowly between swatting flies and walking around. A meal in the restaurant was the highlight of the day, as by evening it was unlikely that we would be making a move just before dark.

This was the third day in Ukhdud now, and not a sign of moving even one millimetre. I had serious thoughts of driving back to Najran and seeing if Ali could help in any way.

Suddenly there was a cloud of dust and a Toyota 4 x 4 roared into view and stopped by my truck. It was the same two Bedouins I had met at the palace. We shook hands and said "Salaam alaykum" to each other. I indicated driving off, but got a shake of the head and was told bukra.

A fly buzzing round woke me up early the next day, which was just as well. It gave me time to drink a cup of coffee and to splash water over my face. The Bedouin's 4 x 4 turned up earlier than expected, so I started the engine to build the air up ready to move off. An Army 6 x 6 came by shortly afterwards and stopped in a cloud of dust. At a quick glance the six soldiers looked even younger than before. They were certainly not the same men and were late teenagers at best. Also, I noticed, there were no goats in the back this time! Within no time at all, we moved off out into the wide open desert. Having done two trips already I was getting very confident about the journey ahead.

It was good going to start with, but there was no sign of any previous tyre marks. We seemed to be going even further south this time. At least the going was better with less soft sand. We made a halt for midday prayers then we hung around for a couple of hours in the hot listless air. At least when we were on the move it made a breeze, even if it was scorching hot. There were always long stops at midday, so maybe the Arabs do use the sun to find the right direction to go.

We missed the outcrop of rocks I was getting used to seeing, and so I had no clue as to where we were.

After getting slowed down by softer sand, but not quite getting stuck, we came to the Bedouin encampment with the well.

It was only half past four and there were still over three hours before dark, but it looked as if we were staying there for the night. There seemed to be a lot more flies about than usual – I expect the flies like what the camels leave behind. It was too hot to close the windows, or to go for a walk, so I just had to grin and bear it. I hate flies! With nothing to do but sweat in the heat of the day, the time dragged by. Remembering "keep a low profile", I did not think it a good idea to visit the Bedouin encampment. I had no doubt they would be hospitable, but just the thought of camel's milk put me off.

The sun seemed to take forever to go down, but once over the horizon it got dark very quickly. At last there were no flies now, and I hoped the mosquitoes preferred camels to me! At least the engine had had time to cool off. It was deathly quiet, as I was some way from the encampment.

I had another fitful night's sleep, waking up with the sunrise. I was also woken by people talking at the well which was only a hundred meters away. They were filling a cut-in-half truck inner tube that was on the back of a pickup. Once it was full of water they drove off back to the encampment.

Then, eventually, there were signs of getting on the move when the Army truck came into view, followed by the Toyota 4 x 4. For a while I thought I'd been forgotten as they started to drive right past me. However I had the air built up ready for the off. To be on the safe side I had parked to the east of the encampment so they had to come this way to get to Sharawrah. Barely slowing down as they passed me by, off they went in a cloud of dust leaving me to follow.

There was still no sign of the rock outcrops to our left, not even the high dunes of the Empty Quarter. The going was mostly fairly hard, with a few small rocks to go round, but I had no complaints. We came across some tracks in the sand going our way. With softer looking sand on either side, there was little choice but to follow the tracks.

Going over a rise and down towards a wadi, the track ahead was barred by an old tyre and a small branch from a tree. At right angles there was a line of trees following the course of the dried up river, leaving just this one gap to cross over the dip. Under another tree on the other side of the wadi sat two formidable Bedouins with rifles. The pathetic road block could have been driven through at a push, but it did not seem like a good idea, as a 4 x 4 jeep was close by on the other side. And they did have guns!

I stopped 20 metres short to take stock of the situation. Being this far south we must be in Yemen. The two soldiers in my cab stayed put, they looked more worried than I was. The Army truck behind had two soldiers standing in the back of their vehicle, so we could make a show of force if necessary. My two Bedouins walked past me to the wadi and stopped. After a few minutes they were invited to join the other two.

For over an hour they talked over a glass of chai. At one point the exchanges got quite heated, and I was beginning to fear the worst. One of my Bedouins came back to my truck and spoke to me in Arabic. I did not have a clue what he meant until he made the shape of a piece of paper. I showed him the letter I had been given by the prince in Najran. He took it from me and went back to join the other Bedouins. As soon as the other Bedouins read my letter, they showed smiles and nods of understanding. Every bit of wasteland desert belongs to one tribe or another, and it was possible we were entering their territory.

I thought I saw something change hands and shortly after we were waved through with a smile and a wave with their rifles.

"Phew," I thought.

The barrier, if you could call it that, was moved to one side and with my letter given back to me we moved off. We drove past a couple of very rough mud huts amongst some trees and then out into the desert once more. That was a close encounter, to say the least. All that trouble to get the letter from the prince! I had not thought that it meant much. Now I knew it gave me a safe passage through even hostile places. It was much more important than I had realised.

After an hour of fairly good going, I noticed the Army truck was no longer behind me. I waited awhile for it, while the Bedouins in their 4 x 4 just carried on driving off into the distance. We were really split up now. I made a wide U-turn and backtracked my distinctive imprint in the sand. A dot in the shimmering distance turned into our Army truck with the bonnet up. Four soldiers were looking at the engine, but none of them seemed to be mechanically minded.

They had almost flattened the battery trying to get the dead engine to start. I had a look, checking the oil and water, and was unable to see anything broken. Maybe the petrol had evaporated in the carburettor. Old American Army trucks ran on petrol. I checked the fuel tank and it was over half full, so that was not the problem.

One thing I did not have was a set of jump leads, and two more tries to start the engine killed the battery completely. I was not prepared to go deeper into the problem – it could be any number of things. I backed my trailer up to the front of their truck and took off a strap from my load that had doubled up on a big case. By making the tow triple strength, this made it shorter, but three times stronger. The sand was fairly soft as I got back into my cab. So, to get the initial start, I reversed a metre, then drove forward to give it a tug and we were on the move. I felt a few jerks and guessed the driver was trying to do a jump start. If the engine had started I would never know with all the dust blown up behind me, so I reluctantly stopped to see what was what. The engine was not going, and never would as far as I was concerned. I told the driver to not try again and indicated two vehicles and the word "Sharawrah". The tow rope seemed none the worse for the tugging, so off we set again.

The sand was getting softer all the while until eventually I came to a stop. My tyres were buried almost up to the rims; to try to go on would only dig them in deeper. The Bedouins came back at last and started shouting "Yalla, yalla" as if we had stopped for a cup of tea. We were stuck in soft sand, so there was going to be no "yalla, yalla" for a while!

Even with all diff-locks engaged, I barely gained a metre forward. I had two choices. One: take off the trailer and tow the Army truck to a harder surface, which could be kilometres away. I was very reluctant to do that. Two: let my tyres down to the minimum of about 20psi and see if that worked.

This did work for about a hundred metres and then I stopped again in even softer sand. The trailer tyres were digging in quite a bit too as the sand was so soft. With everyone's help I got them to push the small valves in on each tyre to let some air out. Soon all eight trailer tyres were starting to bulge. We all got back in our respective cabs, and I gave it another go. I reversed a metre then gave her the gun in second gear, and this time we kept going. I didn't dare change gear – all the time we were moving forward was good enough for me. Although it was broad daylight I guessed it was not easy for the Army driver to see the back of my trailer with all the dust, so I turned on the side lights for him. It took over an hour before the soft sand turned to gravel and it was safe to stop and put some air back into the soft tyres.

My airline was long enough to reach all my tyres, and with the engine going at a fast tick over, I soon had the six truck tyres back up to a safe 60psi. The trailer tyres had been at 100 before, but I thought pumping them up to 60 would do for now. All was going well at pumping up the tyres until the last but one trailer tyre – it was completely flat. The tyres were tubeless which was handy in a way, but the gap between the rim and the tyre was so big that any air put in was lost. I had no spare and did not want to risk running loaded on the inside tyre only.

The trailer wheel nuts were a different size from my wheel brace, so I was unable to change the wheel anyway. The reason for the difference was due to the trailer being American. Some of the ships from America, which had more delicate cargo, sent it already loaded on a trailer. Most of the damage in the docks was done when goods were being transhipped. I expect the Americans thought the trailers would be sent back, but there was no chance of that happening. The docks were in chaos, mainly for lack of equipment. Most of the ships had to use their own derricks and cranes to unload, which was a slow process.

I had seen the wheels repaired in the winter with a drop of petrol poured into the tyre, then set alight. Woof! and the beading of the tyre is touching the wheel rims. This would be enough to be able to then fill the tyre to the required pressure. There was too much of a risk the trailer would go up in smoke for that here. I had the idea that if I put a tourniquet around the middle of the tyre it would bulge the rims out for me. I dug the sand away from under the flat tyre and took a rope off the load.

The six soldiers were not helping by all chattering, especially when I put the rope twice round the tyre and tied one end to the chassis. The longer end of the rope I put round a hook then used a dolly knot in between the two. A dolly knot gives a three in one pull instead of one on a single rope. The soldiers thought I was trying to tie the wheel up and were indicating the wheel would not go round and all sorts of things. The Bedouins must have thought I had gone mad and, after a lot of shouting at me, got into their 4 x 4 and drove off.

To my disappointment not a lot happened to the tyre, so I loosened the rope, which the soldiers approved. Then I put a second dolly knot in front of the first and pulled it all tight again.

"No, no, no," they were shouting in Arabic.

"Yes, yes, yes," I was saying in English as I pulled with all my might on the now six to one pull. Still nothing happened and I was beginning to feel a bit stupid myself. Out of desperation I put a third dolly knot on the rope, hoping the extra strain would not break it.

Thank goodness this time it worked; the middle of the tyre was pulled in just enough for the rims to almost touch. With a couple of kicks to the tyre as the airline was put on again, suddenly the air inside pushed the rims together. The tyre pumped up and I put the rope back on the load. Doing this pleased the soldiers, who now knew that I had not gone crazy, and we were ready to get going again. It had taken a couple of hours or so and there was no sign of the Bedouins.

At a rough guess I thought Sharawrah could be only a hundred kilometres. The more we drove to the north the more chance of being back in Saudi Arabia. It was late in the day as we set off again and it was soon getting dark. At night you could see the undulations in the sand, but there was a danger of missing a big drop. It was also difficult to see any changes in the surface. At least the driver behind on the short tow rope could see the trailer lights more easily.

I was chugging along at a steady 30kph, with my headlights on full beam, when the two soldiers in the cab suddenly started shouting at me to stop. I had seen a few little piles of stones ahead, which was not unusual, and intended to drive on over them. With the now frantic shouting, I slammed the brakes on. Bang! The Army truck crashed into the back of my trailer.

We all got out of the cab and, with the aid of a torch, I went to see if the driver behind was alright. He was shaken but unhurt, as were his three passengers. There was next to no damage to the front of the Army truck with its big front bumper. A big cross girder on the back of my trailer had taken the full force and there was only some paint knocked off. So there was no damage to speak of.

If I had had to make out an accident report, no one would believe me.

"It was dark and I slammed the brakes on to avoid a graveyard, I was not drunk."

After a lot of gesturing I understood that I had been about to drive over a graveyard. Luckily no small pile of stones had been run over. The nearest was just in front of my truck. From what I heard, it was customary for friends or relatives of the deceased to take the body out into the desert for burial. Nobody else knew where the person was buried, and that was it. With at least 20 piles of stones in front of my truck I was unable to go forward. I got back in the cab, engaged reverse and pushed the Army truck back about 50 metres. That's sorted that out! I had had enough for one day, and was not going any further. What a place to spend the night, in a graveyard!

Checking the position of the North Star in the sky I pointed the truck north east ready for the morning and switched off. I always worried about switching off the engine miles from anywhere or anyone.

"Hopes she starts tomorrow," I thought.

The soldiers had no food and just a few bottles of water. I shared some biscuits and a couple of tins with them, and then I hoped the two in the cab would go with their pals so I could spread out to sleep in my cab. However, I think they were getting scared and seemed to have no intention of getting out. They also liked the Arab music on my radio.

What a pickle! No Bedouin guides, a broken down truck to tow and now I was starting to realise I had six young soldiers to care for. I knew more about the desert than they did! It seemed they were sent with me to get some experience. Well, they were certainly getting that!

For me, that must have been the worst night's sleep ever. I was uncomfortable and kept getting cramp, with the occasional sound of snoring thrown in. Daylight could not come quickly enough. But then when dawn did come, I had to decide what our best course of action would be to sort out this predicament. Staying by the graveyard was not going to help. And there was still no sign of the Bedouins.

I checked the oil and water levels, which were still alright despite the extra work. The faithful engine started first time. I made sure we were all on board and started off into the sun. Allowing for the sun to go round, I tried to keep going north east. There was still no sign of the high sand dunes of the Empty Quarter which should start to show up to my left soon.

I forgot to check how many kilometres we had done. With no landmarks, we did not seem to be getting anywhere!

Just as I was beginning to get worried, though not wanting to let the soldiers in the cab know this, the surface gradually changed. At last the undulating stony surface started rattling under the truck. Before, on the previous two trips, we had always driven at right angles to the undulations and there would be Sharawrah after about 20 kilometres.

On and on I drove, and still no Sharawrah in sight. After 25 kilometres the undulations smoothed out back to sand, so I stopped. Looking at the map I saw that there was nothing but desert for hundreds of kilometres from here to the Indian Ocean. If we had passed Sharawrah there was even less chance of being rescued out here.

Our supply of water was now very low and my few tins of food would only last a day or two between six extra mouths. It was the water shortage that was the main worry. I did not fancy drinking the water in the radiator.

Thinking about where I had gone wrong, the first solution would have been to turn round back onto the undulating stony surface. Thinking I was too far south it seemed a good idea to go at a 45° angle over to the right and hope for the best. There was not a single tyre mark to show any sign of life. Going up and down at an angle was a bit like being on a rough sea. I was more worried about the lives of the soldiers with me than I was for myself. It was completely in my hands to get them to safety.

After nearly 10 kilometres of nothing, and getting really worried, we drove over a slightly higher rise and I saw, to my right, the corrugated top of the asphalt building. The relief I felt was enormous! Again I had nearly gone past my destination, and would have gone back into the unknown. With a big smile I turned towards the ramshackle old corrugated building.

We had arrived safely at Sharawrah! That was all that mattered!

From bad to worse

I was glad to disconnect the tow on the Army truck, and the soldiers in the Army truck were pleased too. The driver was pleased just to have stopped. The four soldiers who had stayed in the Army truck were covered in dust from head to toe. How they got their Army truck repaired was their problem now. I shook their hands and said my good-byes.

Within a couple of minutes I had driven to the air field and parked just a few metres away from the main gate. I was not in the mood to get unloaded straight away as enough had gone wrong that day already. Anyway it was a little too late in the day.

Next morning, after drinking my wake-up cup of coffee, I drove up to the main gates for the last time. I had the usual trouble with the guard who again wanted to see my paperwork. He consulted his colleague in the gate house who seemed to be having trouble with the telephone. Eventually he gave up using the phone, and went off in the direction of the control tower. He took my paperwork regarding authority to travel with him. Luckily I had kept the manifest of my load! It is always a risk giving any paperwork to strangers!

After nearly an hour, the English speaking officer came to the gate house and I was allowed inside. Before the officer left me I managed to get his signature on my manifest as proof of delivery.

I parked next to the pile of crates from my previous deliveries, noticing that none of it had been moved. It did not take long to undo all the straps and ropes and stow them in my big tool box.

There was plenty of time to make another coffee while waiting for the big digger to arrive. The digger driver this time was a big man unlike the previous drivers. He did not drive his machine as well as the others and managed to hit the trailer nearly every time another crate needed to be offloaded. When it came to putting the crates down, each one was unceremoniously dropped on top of all the others. It was a relief to get the last of the crates off, and my fuel drums and spare tyre back onto the trailer.

What an unbelievable mess my delivery looked! There had been all the expense of making it, and shipping it from America just for it to end up like this. The team that would come to assemble the ILS system were in for a shock when they started. At least it was all there, which was something. This time I did not stay next to what I thought of as an embarrassment, and parked on the edge of town nearest to Najran.

I stayed there on the edge of town for two days, and nobody came anywhere near me. Twice a day I walked round Sharawrah and saw no one at all. The Army truck had gone, either repaired or towed away. As a last resort I went back to the air field and asked to see the officer, but I was not even allowed inside. The more I waited, the more I thought about making my own way back to Najran.

For safety's sake it is much wiser to travel with at least one other vehicle. I had a really good look at the map, but it did not help very much, it just showed a lot of sand. I did find the water hole on the map, but it was at least 40 kilometres into Yemen and I wanted to avoid going there. That night I decided that if there was no sign of any help in the morning, I would tackle the return trip on my own. The last five journeys had given me a good insight into what I would be confronting, and it did not seem to me to be that daunting.

The next morning, with still no sign of an escort, I checked all the fuel, oil and water levels. My spare fuel and water drums were securely tied down and the tyres looked alright. The yearning to get back was greater than the desire to stay in Sharawrah for even another day. Besides that, I only had two days drinking water left, and about the same in food supplies. It was the water situation that made my mind up that morning. The only regret was not having my letter from the prince in case I got stopped. I had one last look round and started my engine.

Within a couple of hours I had driven 50 kilometres without any trouble. When the gravel ended and the sand started I found a set of jeep tracks. Keeping these in sight on one side gave me confidence in my new choice of route.

My thinking was to always keep the high sand dunes of the Empty Quarter in view to my right. That way I should stay all the time in Saudi Arabia. If I went too far south and into Yemen there would be easier desert to drive on, but I did not want to risk being seen and stopped by Bedouins or, worse still, the Yemeni Army.

The sand began to get much softer and there were half metre high grass stalks which helped a little with traction. The jeep's trail petered out in places, and the sand got softer. Soon there was no sign of the jeep tracks at all, and I was starting to have my doubts.

Then to my disbelief I saw ahead of me a long mound of sand and grass about five metres high. To my right the mound disappeared into a very steep and high sand dune. There was no way I could get an articulated vehicle over that! To the left the mound got gradually steeper and higher and seemed to go on for as far as I could see.

I got out my cab and climbed to the top of the mound. At the top it went down the other side just as steeply at about 45°. Here there was less grass and the sand looked a little firmer. There was no sign of the jeep tracks anywhere. I was on my own now; not lost, but I did not know exactly where I was anymore.

It was certainly a severe obstacle, but with my trailer empty I thought I could drive the truck over the mound and literally drag the trailer after me.

Looking back on it, maybe I should have transferred my fuel drums and water to the artic unit and left the trailer there. Driving with just the unit I would have had no trouble getting over obstacles like that.

Giving in is not in my nature so, after engaging all the diff-locks, I charged up the steep slope. Two things happened that I did not expect! One was that as the cab got to the top it stayed facing uphill. The other was that the truck stopped even though the engine was still going and in gear. I could not go forward and it would not go back, I was stuck! I looked out of my side window and I could see the front axle was at least two metres off the ground, hanging over the drop on the other side. When I turned the steering wheel the front wheels were spinning in mid-air. Checking the green lights on the dash in the bright sunlight I saw that the middle diff-lock light was not on. I put the gear lever in neutral and tried to engage the central transfer box diff-lock by pushing the button in and out and in again. Still it would not engage. Then I tried it with the engine off but ignition left on, and still I had no luck.

"Maybe the truck being at a 45° angle is stopping it, or it is broken!" I thought.

Getting out of the cab with a three metre drop was not easy. I opened the cab door far enough to get out and climb over the back of the cab. Then I went down to the top of the mound where the two rear axles of the truck were sitting. Looking under the front of the trailer, the two guide rails for the 5th wheel were lined up with the chassis of the trailer. Lucky they were the same width apart and I saw that I was in a straight line. All the weight of the overhanging cab was being taken by the trailer pin. I know they are strong, but they have been known to pull out!

There were no oil leaks under the transfer box, so that was a good sign. Next I walked down the slope in the soft sand and went to the back of the trailer. The crash bar right at the back had dug into the sand by nearly half a metre, so no wonder I could not reverse. I wish I had taken a photo of my truck like that, but when trying to sort out a problem this bad it did not come to mind at the time. With difficulty I got my shovel out of the tool box and dug all the sand away at the back of the trailer. Next I dug some of the sand away from the back of the rear drive wheels of the truck. It was now about midday and I was nearly drowning in sweat with the heat.

Getting into the cab at that angle was even harder, but I managed to climb in and start the engine. Engaging reverse gear, and after a few extra revs of the engine, the truck started ever so slowly to roll back and then even to pick up speed. I was back where I had started, but grateful to be safely off the mound.

It may seem stupid now, but at the time I was so hot and annoyed I gave it another go. This time I double checked that the diff–lock light in the middle of the other two switches was on.

I charged up the mound even faster this time, and the truck seemed to hover in mid–air before starting down the other side. The cab seemed to hang for a moment in mid–air then came down rather hard on the other side. I was over! The trailer bottomed out on the ridge but my momentum dragged it over the top like a naughty boy. I hoped there would be no more obstacles like that, as it must have put a lot of strain on everything.

Soon the sand got softer and the undulations steeper so that I had to drive between two ridges of sand dunes. It was midday and I had no idea if I was going west as intended, or south towards Yemen where I did not want to go.

Now I know why the Bedouins stopped at midday. It was not because of the heat, but to get directions from the sun. According to the map I was about 17° above the Equator, and well below the Tropic of Cancer. Whether I liked it or not, and not wanting to lose valuable daylight hours, I stopped on a downward slope and turned the engine off. There was complete silence!

With all the low gear driving, my fuel was getting low in the main tank. The reserve tank on the tool box was empty, so I would have to use fuel from one of the two drums. Before leaving Najran on the second trip I had bought a five metre length of hose for just such an occasion.

First I checked it was diesel and not water in the drum. By putting most of the hose in the tank, then holding my thumb over the end I pulled a couple of metres of hose out, then jumped down and took my thumb off to see if the fuel would flow.

It didn't! I tried this once more but still with no luck, so I had to resort to what I hated doing most. That was sucking the air out of the hose and trying to get the fuel to flow that way. The art of doing this is to do it without getting a mouth full of diesel. Just as I thought I had succeeded, I got a mouthful of diesel, plus some up my nose. It tastes horrible! The only good thing about it was that the fuel was flowing. I put that entire barrel of fuel into my fuel tank. Despite rinsing my mouth out I still had the dreadful taste of diesel for hours afterwards!

With the sun past its zenith, it was as I suspected – I was going more south than west. I had little choice at the moment as on both sides the sand dunes were still over 50 metres high and very steep with loose sand. It was stiflingly hot with the heat radiating off the sand dunes on either side. Gradually the dunes decreased in height, but the sand got even softer and I ground to a halt.

My only choice was to let a little more air out of the tyres. I dreaded one of those big tyres going flat, so I used the tyre gauge to get an accurate reading of 40psi in each tyre. I got back in the cab hoping this would do the trick, but I only moved forward a few metres and got stuck again. Looking ahead a few hundred metres the sand looked a little firmer.

"If only I could get there," I thought.

Trying to dig my way out was not a good option, so I let another 20psi out of the truck tyres. This was my last resort. With fingers crossed, I reversed a metre then tried again to ride over the soft sand. It worked. I stayed in second gear and soon the engine did not labour as much. Once on the firmer sand I pumped the tyres back up to 60psi, which I knew was much safer. Another hurdle had been overcome.

The soft sand gradually changed to gravel, then was mixed with loose stones. At first I thought it was me, but when giving the engine more revs to change up a gear it seemed to falter. After an hour of undulations, the stones were almost the size of footballs. I did my best to go round the larger boulders but could not help running over a few. It made for a very bumpy ride.

Now I wished I had risked going to the south from the start. That way there were long stretches of really hard sand, and in just a few hours I could have travelled nearly 100 kilometres.

The engine was faltering even more and I could not get more than half of the normal engine speed. I estimated I was not even halfway through the journey. Seeing how bad the surface was here, there was no chance of any vehicles coming this way. I had to keep the truck moving, there was no way I could walk out of here!

In the back of my mind, though, I was wondering how much water it was best to carry if I did have to leave the truck and walk to Najran. I was about halfway, but Najran was busier than Sharawrah and easier to get to. At a guess, 10 litres of water weighing 10 kilos could last three days. Walking at night would be better, cooler for one thing and with the North Star for a guide. Walking on sand is very tiring, and I would be lucky to average four or five kilometres an hour, and this would be a lot less climbing up sand dunes. Allowing for stops and sleep, I should be able to keep going for 12 hours a day, thereby averaging 20 to 30 kilometres a day. At a guess Najran was still a 150 kilometres away. That was five or six days, with a good chance of dying of thirst just before I got there. I did not fancy that!

The stony ground went on and on, and then, as I was going up a slightly steeper rise, the engine stopped! I tried the starter and the engine started, but as soon as I tried to move off it stopped again.

"I don't need this, what on earth is wrong now."

I am not a mechanic, so I only know the rudimentary workings of vehicles. I had a reasonable set of tools to hand but these were just for adjusting the brakes. Unlike petrol engines that need the fuel and electrics to all be working properly, a diesel engine only needs fuel to be pumped into the injectors, there is no carburettor to worry about. So the first thing to do was to look at the fuel supply. I checked the fuel tank, it was three quarters full, and so that was alright. The next things to check were the fuel pump and filters.

To do this I needed to tilt the cab forward. The whole cab is on two hinges at the front of the chassis, and is clamped down onto the chassis at the back of the cab. I moved my tins of food from under the passenger seat and put them in the foot well. When the cab is tilted right forward any loose items can fall onto the inside of the windscreen and possibly damage it.

Just behind the cab there are the two clamps which hold the rear of the cab down onto springs and small shock absorbers. I released the clamps and tried to push the cab forward. It would not move! With the help of a long tyre lever I finally managed to unstick it from the mountings.

The other trucks with the sleeper cabs have a hydraulic ram which tilts the cab, using a hand pump. My truck had only muscle power, and with the truck facing uphill the task needed even more effort. I was sweating profusely and getting through my supply of water quicker than I wanted to. I would have to ration out my supply if possible.

Out of frustration and anger I got my back to the cab and heaved. It started to lift up, and soon I had it on the point of balance. Then the cab started to drop forward under its own momentum! That was so scary! It looked as if the front of the cab was going to crash onto the ground. If it did the screen would break and it would be one hell of a job to pull it back up again. If I could get the cab tilted back again I would just have to hope nothing else was broken and the truck was drivable.

Just as the cab seemed doomed, a thick steel cable stopped it going any further – what a relief! Now I could get to the engine very easily. Everything was very hot to touch. I loosened the joint on the fuel pipe from the fuel pump (known as a lift pump) to the injector pump. The latter pressurises the fuel to the injectors – there is one fuel pipe to each cylinder. If the injector pump goes wrong it needs specialised equipment to reset. That was completely out of my range!

When I worked the small pump lever under the fuel pump, just a small dribble of fuel came out. Either the pump was not working or there was a blockage some-where. Just before the main filters there was a glass filter which was meant to trap water. This was secured by a thumb screw underneath, holding the glass egg cup sized filter on. Carefully I undid the screw that held the glass bowl in place. Diesel fuel smothered my hands and gingerly I removed the filter. If I dropped the slip-pery thing now, it was sure to break on the stones below. Diesel is very slippery like oil, and everything was also very hot! I ignored that!

The filter was full of fine sand – no wonder the en-gine was getting starved! I cleaned it all thoroughly, and, with extra care, put the glass filter back in place. I had no spare if this got broken! This time, using the lever on the fuel pump the fuel poured freely out of the loose joint. I tightened everything up and went to start the engine.

The engine turned over, but would not fire up. I have known it to happen before on diesel engines – it is just a case of air being in the system. By loosening the pipe on each injector, one at a time, and turning the engine over, any air gets pumped out. Luckily the starter motor had a button on the casing to make it work. By the time I got to the forth cylinder the engine tried to start and, as I tightened the loose pipe, away she went. That was like music to my ears, and what a relief! I did not realise it at the time, but to get the engine going again was a really a matter of life or death.

Soon I had the cab back down and locked. With some water from the drum I got the worst of the diesel off my hands. Rubbing my hands in the sand also helped to clean them. I was fed up with driving over stones or in soft sand. With little choice, I decided to take the risk of going into Yemen, with the hope of maybe finding my old tracks. After a while the surface became firmer. Yemen or not this was more like it! I was able to go faster than I had all day!

As the sun sank lower in the west, so I chased after it knowing that was the direction I wanted to go. Then the sun went over the horizon! It was nowhere near sunset yet.

"Where has it gone?" I wondered.

With the glare of the sun in my eyes I had missed a gigantic ridge of sand barring my way. This was not unlike the one I recklessly climbed on the last trip back. With all the mishaps of the day, I was not in the mood to take any more chances. I turned to the right heading towards Saudi Arabia, hoping to find an easy way to climb to the top. Instead, after driving a few kilometres along the base, all I found was an even higher sand dune on my left. Then directly ahead it became totally insurmountable as it linked up with the dunes of the Empty Quarter.

I made a wide U-turn and retraced my steps, going south back towards Yemen again. It was over 30 kilometres before the dune gradually lost height, and a little further before finding a gentler slope to get over the long ridge. Once again I could see the sun, and headed west.

There was no chance of getting to Najran in one day. I was hoping to see the outcrop of rocks, and then I would know I was on the right track. Instead I could see nothing, just empty desert in every direction. The sun was dipping over the horizon like a fiery ball. It was time to stop for the night!

I had noticed that Saudi trucks stop in the desert by parking at right angles to the way of travel. This made a lot of sense, as they would be seen much more easily by passing traffic. At night, Saudi trucks would leave their side lights on.

Apart from their trucks being painted very colourfully, they also liked to fit lots of lights of many colours. I have, on occasion, counted over 50 on one side alone, making over 100 altogether. The trucks look like Christmas trees travelling along, but there is one snag. The law in Saudi Arabia does not stipulate red lights at the rear and white lights at the front. More than once on the road at night, when I thought I was catching up to a truck it turned out to be one coming towards me with red lights on the front. A bit scary that!

I parked for the night facing north, which was at a right angle to any possible traffic. I had not eaten all day, so it was time to raid my larder. I still had the taste and could smell the diesel that had splashed on me earlier. However, there was not much I could do about that till I got back. With the engine turned off, everything was deathly quiet, save for the "tink, tink" of the engine exhaust cooling down. Very soon even that noise stopped. I was all alone!

Looking at my depleted store of food, and so as to still leave a choice, I opened one of two tins of tuna, leaving a tin of beans for another day. I ate my tuna with a few digestive biscuits, and then rounded it off with a coffee. Fantastic!

Just in case it would help, I opened up my map of Saudi Arabia and, with the aid of a magnifying glass and the cab light, studied every detail hoping to find where I might be. For the first time I noticed there were two water holes in Yemen on the previous route I had been taken. Also, the way the Bedouins had taken me through the better desert of Yemen had made the journey more like 400 kilometres, not 300. No wonder my fuel was getting used more than I expected.

After my meal, as I was lying down on the double passenger seat looking up at the starry night through the window, I reflected back on the day just ending. I regretted trying to keep in Saudi Arabia. I considered myself lucky to have got through this far. The best thing was the satisfying feeling of having delivered all three trailers to Sharawrah. I put the BBC World Service on the radio, and did not feel so lonely whilst trying to get to sleep.

Surprisingly, I slept quite well for once and I could have my first coffee of the day with no fear of disturbance. The engine started first time, the air pressure soon built up and I was on the move again.

It was still relativity cool, and I remembered to turn left as soon as I got going. The undulating sandy dunes kept pushing me south, but at least I was on fairly hard sand. I kept my eyes peeled for any signs of life and any tracks in the sand. I drove 40 kilometres in an hour and was able to make good progress.

Then, what I dreaded most, I saw something shimmering in the distance. It was only a dark dot at first, but not wanting to be seen I stopped and got out my binoculars. I still could not make out what it was over to my right, so I drove cautiously over to the left to try and skirt round it. This was easier said than done as the sand became very soft and I had to engage the diff-locks.

If it was a jeep, then it would not take long to reach me.

"What would be best, to stop, or make a run for it?" I was thinking. There was no dust coming my way, so probably no vehicle. I stopped again so that I would not be leaving any signs of moving and checked again with my binoculars now that I was a little nearer. It was my stack of rocks! Well, I was pleased!

I was soon able to disengage the diff-locks and drive on firmer sand. The rocks were further away than I thought, and as I drew closer I made sure there was no one parked nearby. It was still mid-morning, but I was so pleased to be somewhere I recognised I stopped for a coffee to celebrate. Looking at the drawing I had made on the first trip this was more likely the outcrop furthest away from Najran. The next outcrop would help to give a line to get back, but I could not see it yet. All the tyre marks of previous visits had gone. What I did have was the towering dunes of the Empty Quarter to the north, so off I drove again with these in sight. Soon the next outcrop came into view. Again, I made sure there was nobody about. It was nearly midday, and I thought it sensible to stop and let the sun go over the meridian.

I was getting a little excited now, with more certainty about getting back safely. I tried to doze off but too many thoughts were going through my mind. The time dragged by, so I walked round the truck to make sure everything was secure. After an hour and a half, I could not wait any longer and started moving again. I drove steadily, looking out for tracks but still not seeing any. The high sand dunes on my right seemed to get nearer. This area was like when we came back before. The trouble is one sand dune looks very much like another. Somewhere along here on the right was the gap leading into Ukhdud, but I still could not see it. Just as I was having doubts about finding it, there was the gap at last. It went back at an angle which tended to hide it from view until the last moment.

Having a good wash came first, before having a meal, and within 15 minutes I was parked next to my other trailers. Within minutes I was in the water trough, enjoying the best and happiest bath I had had for a long time.

I had only half a bottle of water left, so it had been touch and go and a closer run thing than I would have wished. I took the trailer off and drove into Najran to stock up on food and water. Next was to treat myself to a celebration meal in the restaurant.

"Now what shall I have?" I thought. "How about eating chicken and rice for a change?"

Nearly a goner

The meal was very enjoyable, mainly because it was the first time I could really relax. I got up to pay and was offered a hookah to smoke. Of the 10 tables in the room only three were occupied, all by men. Each had a hookah in the middle of the table which they shared. The nickname of hubble bubble is well founded as that is the noise they make when being smoked. By the time the smoke has been sucked through the water, then along the long hose, the smoke is cool and pleasant. I was tempted for a moment then I remembered the previous occasion when I had smoked a hookah pipe.

It had happened when I was driving along the most boring road in Saudi Arabia, called the pipe line road. About 100 metres on the right of the road when driving towards Al Dammam was the oil pipe line going from the oil fields near the Persian Gulf to Jordan, and eventually to the Mediterranean Sea. The road continues straight for nearly a thousand kilometres and just gets boring.

I saw two heavily loaded trucks parked off the road next to a mud hut, so I pulled over myself to get a cold drink. The two drivers were smoking a hookah and invited me to join them. The smoke was surprisingly cool as I puffed and I watched what looked like charcoal and tobacco on the top redden with each puff.

Then I started to feel a little dizzy! I don't know what was mixed in with the tobacco, but it had the same effect as having a few drinks. No wonder there were so many accidents on this road if some of the drivers were a little stoned.

On the pipe line road it was not unusual to have a truck coming towards you in the middle of the road. With no sign of the other truck moving over I had to pull over onto the dirt on the nearside on more than one occasion in order to avoid a head on collision. So, I had not smoked a hookah since then!

Leaving the restaurant, and getting back in my cab, I was feeling rather full but happy. On the drive back to my trailers, I called in at the garage and filled up with fuel, ready for the long haul back to Jeddah.

Just before reaching my trailers I noticed a cut away in the sand. It was dug to load sheep or goats from a sloping pit. The truck would back down the slope so that the back of the truck was level with the ground. On taking a closer look, I could see the bottom needed digging out where the sides had slid down; otherwise it was just what I needed. It was too late in the day to get anything done, so I watched the sun go down and tried to sleep for what would hopefully be my last night in Najran.

I was up early the next day, with the thought of leaving today and driving along the cool mountain road to Ta'if. I had a quick wake up wash in the water trough, and then my coffee and biscuits for breakfast.

With no dolly or means of towing a second trailer I would have to load two of the trailers onto the third one. A crane could have done the job in half an hour, but with no cranes available I would have to do all the work myself.

I had used all my wooden chocks under the legs of the first two trailers, so I chose one of these trailers first to reverse down the slope. That would give me some spare chocks to use. I had thought of pumping my tyres up to normal 120psi but the sand looked very soft around the pit, so I left the tyres at 60psi for the time being.

Digging out the loose sand in the bottom of the pit was not as easy as I hoped as the sides kept sliding down. All I could do was to make it a little deeper where the trailer wheels would go. I was getting hot already and had not really started yet!

I reversed the trailer down the slope and got out to see how near the back of the trailer was to the bank. It was much too high (40cm higher at the back) to be able to reverse a trailer on to it. To do more digging would be a waste of time and effort. Then I had an idea!

I drove forward a few metres and disconnected the airlines. This would lock the trailer wheels. I reversed back with more force into the bank of sand. It worked! The trailer tyres had dug into the soft sand and now there was only a small gap at the back of the trailer. I wound the trailer legs down on the wooden blocks, but they kept sinking into the sand. After the legs looked more settled, with no more sinking, I was happy to disconnect the trailer and go to get the next one. This was a good start but it was already 10 o'clock and getting hotter every minute. However, stage one was accomplished!

To hook up to the second trailer was easy as it was me that had last used it. With the second trailer on, I drove past the trailer in the pit and carefully and slowly reversed onto the first trailer. The sand was very soft, so I was glad I had not pumped up the tyres on my truck. Once this second trailer was level with the one underneath, I disconnected it and drove round to the front to hook up to the first trailer. The legs had sunk into the sand a bit, but luckily I just managed to drive my unit under and hook up.

As soon as I pulled the two trailers out of the pit, I stopped and secured the wheels of the loaded one with crossed ropes on each wheel. I had seen this done on

Loading the empty trailers

farm tractor transporters, so it must be the way to do it. Stage two was done.

Things were going well. I had never done this before so wanted to get it right. I unhooked the loaded trailer on the road, and went to get the last one. The legs on this one had sunk, and I had to mess about using my spare blocks to raise it enough to reverse under. It was midday by now and I was sweating and panting more than I would have liked. I had a splash in the water trough and this helped to cool me down for a while.

This last trailer was the one I had just brought back from Sharawrah, so first I had to take off the oil drums and spare tyre before reversing it down the ramp. Next I did the same as before by disconnecting the airlines and forcing the trailer down the slope and against the loading bank.

As I wound the legs down, I watched the blocks of wood disappear into the sand again. This was making it so hard. When I thought it had stopped sinking, I unhitched and pulled out to get hooked up to the two trailers.

Half a dozen children, about six to eight years old, stood watching me and making loud comments. Maybe it was because I had no shirt on and that I was only wearing shorts. I took no notice of them as I wanted to get this loading done.

Reversing the loaded trailer onto the one in the pit was successfully accomplished. Just one more hook up to do and the hard work would be done for the day. Or so I thought! At least I was up to stage three.

The legs on the trailer in the pit had sunk even further into the sand with the extra weight. Each trailer weighed about five tons, so the one I wanted to get under now had ten tons loaded on it. The legs were wound down to their maximum, and I had used all the wooden blocks. These were now buried in the sand. I could not even get the rear of my truck under the front of the trailer. So it was out with the shovel again. I dug two ruts where the rear wheels of my truck would need to go.

This was enough to get the front of the trailer onto the rear on my chassis, but not enough for it to slide up the guide rails. Now it was safe to wind the legs up and put something underneath the legs to give them the extra lift needed. I found some heavy flat rocks nearby and positioned them on the now buried wood. With two trailers loaded, the handle for the legs was even harder to turn, even in low gear. (Trailer legs have two gears, high for empty or to raise, and low when any weight is involved, as now.)

I could hardly see for sweat as I wound the legs down onto the rocks. Once the trailer legs were down to the rocks, a lot more effort was needed to turn the handle. The trailer started to very slowly lift up, and the rocks seemed to be holding. Suddenly there was a crunch and a bang! I thought the trailer might tip over onto me if the rock crumbled on my side.

Instead, down at my feet was a half quashed pomegranate that had hit the trailer right in front of my face. One of the children had thrown it at me and they were all having a good laugh at my expense. They made me so angry that I picked up the pomegranate and hurled it back at them with all my might.

It was then that I felt a pain in my chest and I all but blacked out, my knees sagged and I was on all fours on the ground. I hardly remember crawling to my cab. Somehow I got in the cab and just slumped over the wheel. I was soaked in sweat, panting, and could feel my heart thumping away. For 10 minutes I never moved, not able to focus on anything, not even able to think coherently. All my strength had gone.

Taking a long drink of water helped to revive me a little. Luckily when I had last gone shopping I had bought a kilo of tomatoes. I ate most of these with lots of salt. It was at least half an hour later that I felt revived enough to put the kettle on and make a cup of tea with lots of sugar added. After drinking the tea I started to feel much better. My pulse was just about back to normal – it had been racing away at first.

I must have frightened the children, as they had all run off. I had certainly frightened myself. I had not only completely overdone it in the heat of the day, I had nearly killed myself!

"Just a few more turns of the handle should do the trick," I thought as I got out for one final effort.

When I looked down, even the rocks were starting to sink now. This was ridiculous, so taking a chance it might work, I got back into the cab. I started the engine and put her into reverse gear. The wheels started to spin slowly as the truck tried to go backwards. With every turn the wheels started to dig down into the sand. I heard a loud grinding sound and the back of my truck lurched down. Then, as I looked in the mirror, I could see the trailer starting to rise up as my truck reversed under it. This was just what I had hoped would happen. I heard the reassuring "clunk" as the 5th wheel clamped onto the trailer pin.

All I had left to do now was to roll the fuel drums and spare tyre onto the trailer and tie them down. Using all the ropes and straps that I had left, I put extra fixings over the top trailer. The last thing I wanted to happen on the way back to Jeddah was that if I had to brake hard I would have the trailers slide forward onto the top of my cab.

In my haste to get away I nearly forgot that the tyres needed to be pumped up to normal pressure. The truck tyres did not take too long, but the eight trailer tyres were a bit awkward, particularly trying to pump up the inner tyres.

At last I was ready to leave. I had given the loading a lot of thought beforehand, but had not thought it would take this long, or prove to be so difficult. It seemed as if it had been an even hotter day than usual, but maybe the extra manual work had given that impression. I had one last dip and soak in the water trough that had been such a welcome luxury.

It was time for a celebration meal. In the back of my food store was a tin of beans and pork sausages saved since the American in the telephone exchange had given it to me. I heated the tin up on the stove until it bubbled. Then eating it with a tea spoon I savoured every mouthful. At that moment it even beat chicken and rice.

One last duty before I left was to say goodbye to Ali. Without his help and friendship I doubt if I would have been able to do the job at all. Both his Toyota 4 x 4 and his old Chevvy were parked outside so hopefully he was at home. I knocked on his door and was glad to see him again. I pointed at my truck, now all ready to go, and told him, "Searra Jeddah."

He understood that I was leaving and gave me a firm hug and I guess he said in Arabic, "Have a good journey, God be with you."

I said, "Shukran" ("thank you") a few times.

I never did learn the Arabic for goodbye, so said,

"Allas malla douk" which is goodbye, but in Turkish.

It was quite an emotional moment and I have to admit I had a tear or two in my eye. As I walked back to my truck I turned round and we both waved to each other for the last time. We had only known each other for less than a couple of months, but somehow it seemed longer than that.

I would miss the trips to Najran to get a six pack of beer between us. That had been the fun part of the last two months. That and having a good soak in the water trough!

Return to Jeddah

After all the effort of loading the trailers, it was great to relax behind the wheel, and to drive on a tarmac road again. The tempting right turn to the cool mountains was just ahead, and what a joy it was to turn right and to go up that road. Very soon the gentle climb began. There were quite a few sweeping bends on the climb up into mountains. Within half an hour it was already noticeably cooler and after an hour I was at the top where it was cooler still at 90°F.

I had all of the next day to get back to Jeddah, so I decided that at the first good place I found I would pull over for the night. There were not many laybys or good places to stop as I always like to pull well off the road.

In Saudi Arabia, as in most Middle East countries, if you are stationary and another vehicle crashes into you then you are in real trouble, with a possible jail sentence or expulsion. The thinking is that if you had not been there, then the accident would not have happened, so it's your fault!

Eventually I came across an open space that had once been a road building compound, so I pulled in and parked in the corner. Khamis Mushayt was not far up the road. Having driven nearly 200 kilometres I felt I had done well for one day.

Just to breathe in the cooler air was a pleasure as I walked round checking that all the straps and ropes were still tight. A couple of ropes needed tightening up, but the trailers had not moved which was the main thing.

On way back to Jeddah with all three trailers

I think that the road had not been built very long. The road surface was in excellent condition and very smooth. There were not any little roadside shops or restaurants, but I think that was because of the lack of traffic. It was possible to drive for half an hour and see only one or two vehicles passing in the other direction.

It got quite cold overnight, and I was glad to get up and make a cup of coffee. There was some mist coming up from the valley on the Red Sea side but this soon dispersed. I had a walk round to check on everything and was glad to get back in the cab, out of the chill air. It was not shorts and T-shirt weather up here. It was good to start the engine and break the complete silence, and soon I was on the road again. With the lack of roadside places to eat, I looked out for a place when I got to Abha. I managed to order bread and honey by going into the kitchen and seeing what they had, then pointing to what I wanted. It was a change from chicken and rice. You can have too much of a good thing sometimes.

Soon I was back on the road again and enjoying every kilometre of the rugged, dark, mountainous scenery. Going down one long, gentle slope the stones in the road warned me of the unbuilt bridge ahead. There were a couple of workmen about but no sign of the bridge being built. Just to be safe, I got out and checked all the ropes and straps were tight. It was very steep and bumpy going down, and about the same going up the other side. The stream had dried up which made things easier. After getting to the top and parking, I checked the trailers and was pleased nothing had moved.

By mid–afternoon I had reached Ta'if and was very tempted to go on down the escarpment and back to Jeddah. However, I had endured nearly two months of what was to me extreme heat and the lure of another cool night's sleep was too great, so I pulled off the road where you can look over the edge towards Mecca. There were a couple of trucks parked up but none that I recognised.

I had an even better night's sleep, mainly because it was not quite so cold but just right. The last 24 hours had restored me to my old self. I could think a lot more quickly and clearly, compared to when I was in the desert.

The next morning, after a cup of coffee, I got onto the road early and was soon going down the long escarpment road and back to the hot desert. As I approached the bottom of the long drag down, I saw an amazing sight. What used to be scrubland, with more dead than alive clumps of bush, was now all the colours of the rainbow. The whole desert had sprung into flower. In quite a few places the road had a thick covering of sand and gravel, and I had to slow right down to go over it. There had obviously been a flash flood recently.

By ten-thirty I was back at our villa in Jeddah. I parked round the back and was surprised that there was nobody about. With my signed delivery note in my hand, I triumphantly walked into the villa hoping to get praised for a job well done.

I walked into the traffic office where the manager was sitting behind a desk. Before I could say a word he looked up and said, "Where the hell have you been?" With that welcome I was not in the mood to explain things just then. So I said nothing and just turned round and walked out of the office, leaving the delivery note on his desk.

After getting a cold drink from the fridge and sitting in our lounge area I realised I had been a long time, but could not see what I could have done to make it any quicker. The manager came in and we talked over what had taken so long. I tried to explain all the delays I had encountered. The actual driving time over the desert on the three journeys had taken 11 days; the other 40 odd days had been lost waiting for the Bedouin guides or to see the prince. My explanation was accepted, even if not fully understood.

I asked about all the flowers I had seen around Mecca, and he told me there had been a rain storm a few days before, with lots of roads flooded.

I also asked where all the other drivers were, and was told they were all out on the road as they had been very busy. This manager was a relative of the owner and was normally at work flying DC-10s around the world. The airline had given him six months off for some reason, and he was working with us in Jeddah for something to do. One of the reasons why they were so busy was that he had gone to the steel compound to ask how many tons of 17mm steel rods were there for sale. The answer was 4,000 tons, so he bought the lot. This pleased the steel yard owner and arrangements were made to leave it in his yard until required.

Not long after that an unfortunate accident happened to the barge that was bringing in another consignment of 17mm rods. It sank in the depths of the Red Sea during a freak squall. To make matters worse for the steel yard owner, it was already paid for before delivery. The 17mm steel rods were very much sought after for many of the building projects going on everywhere. White Trux could not only charge more because they had the monopoly, but they insisted it all had to be delivered on White Trux vehicles. That was a very clever business move I thought!

On a lighter note, I was told that my three months were up and I could fly home the next day. A ticket had been arranged and my flight was for tomorrow afternoon.

After finishing my drink I went out to my truck. I took off all the ropes and straps from the trailer, and left them tidy in the tool box. I had very few personal bits in the cab, but took out what little I did own, plus all my music tapes. I had no souvenir of Sharawrah except a little sand on the floor of the cab. They could keep that!

The next day I packed my suitcase, including the 50 new music tapes I had bought at the souk in Jeddah. By eleven in the morning I was ready to go. The time seemed to drag by, but then there was a commotion outside.

A fully loaded Saudi truck pulled up outside our villa with smoke pouring out of the back wheel. Within a short time the smoke turned to flames. The wheel bearing must have broken and, with the heat generated, this had set fire to the grease in the bearing. Two of us rushed out and threw a bowl of water over the rear wheel hub. The flames died and there was smoke again. Just when we thought we had solved the problem, the hub burst into flames again. It took half a dozen more douses of water for the flames to finally stop and the bearing to start cooling down safely.

Just before leaving in a taxi to go to the airport, the manager gave me a letter asking if I could go on the flight deck during the flight. The flight was on time and soon I was on board, looking forward to getting home. Once we had taken off, I gave the cabin steward my letter and was told it should be alright once we were over the Alps. With an hour to go before touchdown I was called forward and allowed into the cockpit. What a disappointment!

The captain said hello as he relaxed with the plane on autopilot. He was smoking a rather smelly pipe and there was tobacco ash all over the floor. I have always been fascinated by dials and switches but that was a disappointment too. The dials were all covered in dust and two of them still had their serial number in chalk on the glass. I kept the dash on my truck cleaner than that, even in the desert. It only takes a regular wipe over with a cloth to keep it clean. I was glad to get back to my seat!

We made a good landing at Heathrow, and I was soon in customs explaining why I had so many music tapes. I told the customs man I had taken them out to Saudi Arabia to play while I was driving on the long lonely roads. I don't think he really believed me, but he gave me the benefit of the doubt. I was grateful for that as I had only paid a pound per tape. Some were selling at five times that price in England. Eventually, he stamped my suit case and I could go. I found out later that I should have paid import duty or VAT or something.

It was great to be home again, but what a contrast to being out in the desert of southern Saudi Arabia. Thinking back over the last couple of months, it all seemed to be a bit of a dream. I will always remember Ali and I have the photos of the trips I made. I now know where Sharawrah is and how to get there. It's not easy! It was an exciting experience and one I will never forget.

There was only one downside to the whole adventure. After my month at home, I flew back to Jeddah to do another three months' work. However, unbeknown to me, while I had been doing my upmost to get the three trailers to Sharawrah as quickly as possible, my wife back in England feared the worst as she did not hear from me. Phoning White Trux gave her no news of where I was as they did not know where I was either. Not doing things by halves, she got on to the Foreign Office and asked them to find me.

They could not have looked in the right places; it seems Sharawrah is a good place to hide from the authorities. White Trux were not impressed with being pestered by the Foreign Office, and I was told my employment would terminate at the end of the three months.

Nevertheless, I enjoyed those last three months. This time I had a Volvo F88 with a sleeper cab. It did not seem like autumn, except it was a little cooler, and there was plenty of money to be earned.

The desert still holds a fascination for me, despite the flies and the scorching heat. It has a beauty of its own with its soft shapes, yet harsh way of life. Now, with the dual carriage highways built across the desert, it will never be so difficult to get anywhere in Saudi Arabia again.

Hardback
£19.95
Each

AT WORK SERIES

PATRICK DYER

HARDBACK

ISBN: VARIOUS

About the Books

This unique series of highly illustrated hardback books feature truck models from DAF 2800 to Volvo F12 and everything in-between, a real treat for the enthusiast.

DAF at Work: 2800, 3300 & 3600 - 9781906853372

Ford Transcontinental at Work - 9781908397102

Seddon Atkinson at Work: 400, 401 &4-11- 978190397430

Scania at Work: LB110, 111, 140 & 141 - 9781905523993

Volvo F10 & F12 at Work: 1977-83 - 9781908397614

Volvo F88 & F89 at Work Second Edition - 9781908397157

Scania 112 &142 at Work – 9781908397874

For our full range of products visit
www.oldpond.com or
call **0114 240 9930**
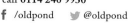 /oldpond @oldpond

BEYOND THE BOSPHORUS

DAVE BOWERS

HARDBACK

ISBN: 9781910456026

About the Book

In this book Dave Bowers tells with humour and insight the amazing stories of people driving to Middle East destinations, battling against all the odds to deliver their loads.

Illustrated with photographs of the drivers and vehicles taken at the time, Beyond the Bosphorus records what it was like for ordinary HGV drivers to get involved in something so dramatically different from their everyday working lives in the UK. It will be of interest to lorry drivers, general vehicle enthusiasts and also those with a historical and social interest in the Middle East alike.

About the Author

Dave Bowers has been writing features on trucks, the road haulage industry, travel, history, classic cars, tractors and repairing vehicles for a number of magazines, including Truck and Driver, Trucking, Heritage Commercials and Classic Truck for over 20 years.

For our full range of products visit
www.oldpond.com or
call **0114 240 9930**
f /oldpond   🐦 @oldpond

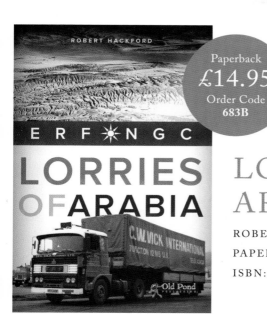

Paperback
£14.95
Order Code
683B

LORRIES OF ARABIA

ROBERT HACKFORD

PAPERBACK

ISBN: 9781908397935

About the Book

Published in 2015 this is an account of the magnificent ERF NGC machine hauling articulated road-trains over the Saudi mountains in Trans-Arabia livery. A treat for any Middle East trucking enthusiast.

This book is a tribute to ERF's world-class long-hauler, especially the Middle-East examples, and to those who drove them. What did the ERF NGCs look like? How well did they perform? Where did they venture? What were they like to drive and to live in? And where did they stand in ERF's contribution to Britain's place in the history of the TIR-trail?

About the Author

Robert Hackford is a retired teacher and long-haul trucker. He is author of Kamyonistan Quartet (a novel, Athena Press) and has had many articles published in trucking magazines.

For our full range of products visit
www.oldpond.com or
call 0114 240 9930
f /oldpond 🐦 @oldpond

Old Pond
PUBLISHING

DVD PAL
£17.95
Order Code
213D

DESTINATION DOHA

TONY SALMON

DVD PAL

ISBN: 9781906853143

About the Book

Two "World About US" programmes broadcast in 1977 in which we meet truckers driving over 5,000 miles and 11 countries between Britain and the Arabian Gulf.

Doha, the capital of Qatar on the Arabian Gulf is 5,000 miles from London with 11 countries to travel through and 23 customs posts on the way. Blizzards in Austria, sandstorms in Syria: broken-down trucks to repair and bogged-down trucks to dig out of the sand.

This double DVD set contains both parts of the original programme. You'll see that for these Astran international drivers their work was more than just a job – it was a way of life with a series of adventure, winter and summer, ice-cold and desert-hot.

Running time is 98 minutes.

For our full range of products visit
www.oldpond.com or
call **0114 240 9930**
f /oldpond   @oldpond

Unipower and Faun working in harmony.

Macks in action down under.

INTERNATIONAL HEAVY HAUL 2

74 MINUTES

DVD PAL

ISBN: 9781908397942

DVD PAL
£16.95
Order Code
324D

About the DVD

In International Heavy Haul TWO we travel to four different parts of the world to bring you features showing heavy haulage at its most impressive.

The first film looks at the transport of two 130-tonne bridge beams in Australia. We see the crews starting their day's work in a remote layby on the Great Northern Highway between Perth and Port Hedland, and accompany them for some distance - excellent in- cab footage is included. Traction is provided by Mack-ballasted tractors with the beams supported front and rear on 7&8 row bogies.

In the second feature we move to South Africa. Here we were privileged to witness the movement of a 356-tonne transformer, which was being carried on a girder frame supported by 24 rows of axles. Motive power is provided by three 8x8 Tractomas ballasted tractors and a rebuilt 6x4 Pacific.

For our full range of products visit
www.oldpond.com or
call **0114 240 9930**
f /oldpond **🐦** @oldpond